T0358695

# NARRATIVE AND SIMILE
# FROM THE GEORGICS
# IN THE AENEID

# MNEMOSYNE

## BIBLIOTHECA CLASSICA BATAVA

COLLEGERUNT

W. DEN BOER · A. D. LEEMAN · W. J. VERDENIUS

BIBLIOTHECAE FASCICULOS EDENDOS CURAVIT

W. J. VERDENIUS, HOMERUSLAAN 53, ZEIST

SUPPLEMENTUM QUINQUAGESIMUM OCTAVUM

WARD W. BRIGGS, jr.

## NARRATIVE AND SIMILE
## FROM THE GEORGICS
## IN THE AENEID

LUGDUNI BATAVORUM E. J. BRILL MCMLXXX

# NARRATIVE AND SIMILE FROM THE GEORGICS IN THE AENEID

BY

WARD W. BRIGGS, JR.

LEIDEN E. J. BRILL 1980

ISBN 90 04 06036 7

*MEIS PARENTIBUS*

# TABLE OF CONTENTS

# PREFACE

The present work is an expansion of part of my doctoral dissertation done at the University of North Carolina at Chapel Hill in 1974.

My debts are as uncountable as those of anyone who uses the Virgilian bibliography. The absence of some important works from my Bibliography does not mean that I have ignored them: indeed, many have been at hand constantly in my study of the subject. The abundant learning in the scholarship of Cartault, Norden, and R. D. Williams in particular have been of inestimable value. Special gratitude of a more personal kind must be extended to W. A. Camps for initial encouragement in the study of Virgil, to Berthe M. Marti and Kenneth J. Reckford for their careful reading and generous suggestions that helped me pare down the extensive early drafts of the dissertation, and to Catherine Castner for her patient assistance and support at every stage of the project.

The greatest obligation of all is to my director, Brooks Otis, who suggested the topic, clarified much that was obscure, and let me guide this creation home to its present form. It was not the least of his many special gifts that his titanic wisdom and supreme humanity were best satisfied when they helped others uncover answers for themselves, answers in which he never failed to be interested.

I am grateful also to the University of South Carolina Research and Productive Scholarship Fund for grants to support the publication of this book.

Such faults as remain here, despite the best efforts of many friends and colleagues, are my own.

*Columbia, S.C.*
*November 26, 1978*

# ABBREVIATIONS

References to some works are abbreviated as follows:

Austin, I                  *P. Vergili Maronis Aeneidos Liber Primus*, ed. R. G. Austin, Oxford, 1971.

Austin, II               *P. Vergili Maronis Aeneidos Liber Secundus*, ed. R. G. Austin, Oxford, 1964.

Austin, IV               *P. Vergili Maronis Aeneidos Liber Quartus*, ed. R. G. Austin, Oxford, 1955.

Austin, VI               *P. Virgili Maronis Aeneidos Liber Sextus*, ed. R. G. Austin, Oxford, 1977.

Büchner                K. Büchner, *P. Vergilius Maro: Der Dichter der Römer*, Stuttgart, 1966 (= *RE* VIIIA, cols. 1021ff.)

Conington-Nettleship    *P. Vergili Maronis Opera: The Works of Virgil*, ed. J. Conington; III, 3rd ed. rev. by H. Nettleship London, 1883.

Heinze                R. Heinze, *Virgils Epische Technik*, 3rd ed., Berlin, 1915.

Huxley                *Virgil: Georgics I and IV*, ed. H. H. Huxley, London, 1963.

Otis                  B. Otis, *Virgil: A Study in Civilized Poetry*, Oxford, 1963.

Richter                *Vergil Georgica*, ed. W. Richter, Munich, 1957.

Wigodsky             M. Wigodsky, *Vergil and Early Latin Poetry*, Wiesbaden, 1972.

Wilkinson            L. P. Wilkinson, *The Georgics of Virgil*, Cambridge, 1969.

G. Williams          G. Williams, *Tradition and Originality in Roman Poetry*, Oxford, 1968.

Periodical abbreviations are those of *L'Année Philologique*.
The text of Virgil is that of M. Geymonat (Turin, 1973).

# INTRODUCTION

> He who resolves never to ransack any mind but his own,
> will soon be reduced, from mere barrenness, to the
> poorest of all imitations; he will be obliged to repeat
> himself, and to repeat what he has before often repeated.[1]

Virgil's work is surely not barren of the gifts of other minds. But can we say that Reynolds' dictum, that self-imitation is "the poorest of all", is true in the case of the *Georgics* and the *Aeneid*? It is the contention of this book that it is not.

The repetitions with which I am concerned have, like the famous half-lines of the *Aeneid*, no counterpart, either in frequency or length, in extant classical literature. I emphasize that I am speaking of extant work. Surely some writer must have composed poems of different genres at some time in antiquity that may well have had similar repetitions. But if such works existed, we do not have them now. Moreover, we do not have enough of the poetry of any one man to make comparable judgements on repetitions between poems of the same genre, with a few exceptions. Apart from some isolated and infrequent examples (most seemingly unconscious), the evidence points to a studied antipathy to such a practice.

Of course, one can find occasional idiosyncratic echoes like:

ἔστιν δὲ τοῦτο οὐ καθόλου, ὥσπερ καὶ ᾿Αγάθων λέγει: τάχ᾽
ἄν τις εἰκὸς αὐτὸ τοῦτ᾽ εἶναι λέγοι, βροτοῖσι πολλὰ τυγχάνειν
οὐκ εἰκότα.

Arist. *Rhet.* 2.24.1402a8

ἔστιν δὲ τοῦτο καὶ εἰκὸς ὥσπερ ᾿Αγάθων λέγει, εἰκὸς γὰρ
γίνεσθαι πολλὰ καὶ παρὰ τὸ εἰκός

Arist. *Poet.* 18.1456a

Such parallels occur throughout any literature and have the character of a cliché. Despite the best efforts of the writer, they will be found in literature as easily as in conversation and do not seriously affect our consideration of the subject matter.

The focus of this book is not on commonplaces of diction but rather on the practice that was part of every Roman's education, that of *retractatio* (or ἀγών), a "competition" in the sense that one

---

[1] Sir Joshua Reynolds, *Discourse to the Students of the Royal Academy*, 10 Dec. 1774.

attempts to achieve perfection by improving on passages borrowed
from earlier writers.[2] This practice seems to the modern, post-
romantic mind no less than plagiarism, but the testimony of the
ancients, especially Horace, shows that the skillful borrowing from
great masters is an estimable accomplishment, more so than pure
originality.[3]

Among the Greeks, there was a chestnut of unknown history
found in many writers and codified by Empedocles: "καὶ δὶς γάρ,
ὃ δεῖ, καλόν ἐστιν ἐνισπεῖν."[4] Some use this as an excuse for repetition,
others for the opposite.[5] The basic idea is that once an idea has been
perfectly expressed, there is no point in trying to do it another way.
Theon of Alexandria, in his *Progymnasmata*, refutes the notion,
citing passages in Homer (*Od.* 18.136-137) and Archilochus (68D)
to show that no two poets ever describe the same thing in the
same way for the same purpose.[6] He then notes, with examples,
how carefully Demosthenes altered his expressions for any given
statement. For example, Demosthenes repeats an identical thought
in speeches given three years apart, to different audiences:[7]

---

[2] The implications of "retractatio" in estimating Virgil's originality was
the special concern of A. M. Guillemin, *L'originalité de Virgile: étude sur la
méthode littéraire antique*, Paris, 1931, 5-9, 125-154. See also, W. F. J. Knight,
*Roman Vergil*, London, 1966, 101-107, G. Williams, Ch. V (esp. 255-260),
and, more generally, A. Reiff, *Interpretatio, imitatio, aemulatio. Begriff und
Vorstellung literarischer Abhängigkeit bei den Römern*, Dissertation, Cologne,
Würzburg, 1959. See Wigodsky, 2-15 for an account of imitation and allusion
in Virgil (primarily short phrases).

[3] See Hor. *A.P.* 128-142. One must always keep in mind Virgil's view
of imitation, "verum intellecturos facilius esse Herculi clavam quam Homero
versum subripere." (*Vita Donati* 46).

[4] Fr. 25D.

[5] The saying is used to censure repetition by Pindar, *Nem.* 7.104, Soph.
*Phil.* 1238, Aristoph. *Clouds* 546, Plato *Phaedrus* 235A and to defend or
even extol it in the Paroemiographers, Plato *Gorgias* 498E, *Phil.* 59E, *Laws*
956E, 6.754C. See P. Friedländer, Δὶς καὶ τρὶς τὸ καλόν, *TAPA* 69 (1938),
375-380.

[6] L. von Spengel, *Rhetores Graeci*, Leipzig, 1854, II, 62-63.

[7] A. B. Cook, "Unconscious Iterations" *CR* 16 (1902), 149. Isocrates,
in his six forensic speeches of 402-403 B.C. (if they are genuine), repeats
himself deliberately and acknowledges it in speeches that were never intended to be delivered, only studied (see *Phil.* 90-93). He even gives a defence
of the repetition in *Paneg.* 145-149 in discussing the statement in the *Anabasis*
that Persia is weak. And even though he had written the *Panegyricus* 30
years earlier, he nevertheless felt obliged to justify the repetition in *Phil.* 93.
In the *Antidosis*, after borrowing from earlier speeches and asking an ima-
ginary clerk to read from them, he says that he has grown feeble in his old
age and cannot say at length what he would like and so must repeat. (59)

σὺ δὴ μὴ λέγ' ὡς γέγονε τοῦτο πολλάκις, ἀλλ'
ὡς οὕτω προσήκει γίγνεσθαι.

*Androt.* 7

μὴ δὴ τοῦθ' ὑμῖν ἐᾶτε λέγειν, ὡς γέγονεν, ἀλλ'
ὡς ἔστι δίκαιον γίγνεσθαι,...

*Aristoc.* 98

and Cicero gives us in his didactic works,

imago [est] animi voltus, indices oculi...quare oculorum
est magna moderatio

*De Orat.* 3.221-322

tum oculorum est quaedam magna moderatio; nam ut imago est
animi voltus, sic indices oculi.

*Orator* 60

"Surely unique in history" [8] is the repetition in the Second *Philippic*
of a statement made 20 years earlier in the Fourth *Catilinarian* in
which Cicero says that a man who lived to be consul could not
complain of an early death:

Si quid obtigerit, aegro animo paratoque moriar. Nam
neque turpis mors forti viro potest accidere neque immatura
consulari.

*Cat.* 4.2.3

Etenim si abhinc annos prope viginti hoc ipso in templo
negavi posse mortem immaturam esse consulari, quanto verius
hunc negabo seni?

*Phil.* 2.119

In asserting the continuity of his willingness to die for the Republic,
he repeats at once a stylistic felicity and a thematic statement,
much as we saw his model, Demosthenes, do.[9]

Repetitions of this kind are rare in poetry, also, but the most
significant turns up in one of the sources of the *Georgics*, Hesiod.
In the proem to the *Works and Days*, Hesiod addresses the Pierian
Muses, mentions the greatness of Zeus and how he will praise him,

---

[8] G. C. Richards s.v. "Cicero", *Oxford Classical Dictionary*², Oxford,
1968, 190.

[9] Although Atticism was characterized by repetition of phrases in the
style of the older Greek orators, it is not a significant rhetorical feature of
Roman declamation, nor the speeches in Virgil (who was trained by the
Atticist Quintilius Varus), nor the speeches of the historians (F. W. Walbank,
*Speeches in the Greek Historians*, Oxford, 1966, 13).

and ends with the promise that he will teach his perfidious brother
Perses to speak the truth (10). In the proem to the *Theogony*, at
line 28, he likewise speaks of telling the truth, but there is a difference. In the former, he is trying to change his brother from a
liar into an honest man; in the latter, he is referring to his own
desire as a poet not to tell "false things [i.e. myths] *as if* they
were true, but the truth itself".

*Works* 11-26 mentions the wars of heaven, the same strife that
is recounted at greater length in the *Theogony*, 225ff. But in the
*Works*, Hesiod speaks philosophically about the right life for man;
in the *Theogony*, he is describing the genealogies of heaven.

Both the invocations and the wars reflect themes the poet felt
to be important enough for inclusion in both poems. But it should
be noted that the repetition of the battle serves a different purpose.
In the *Works*, the strife in heaven mirrors the strife of rival crafts-
men in that competition improves the product (24-26); in the
*Theogony*, the series of strifes prepares for the reign of Zeus.

The Prometheus-Pandora-Jar of Evils Episode (*Works* 42-105)
may be compared with the account in the *Theogony* of the crime of
Prometheus and the origin of the first woman (507-616). Both tell
roughly the same story, and both end with a similar line, but
again there is a fundamental difference: the story in the *Works*
no longer describes woman as originally evil *per se*, but rather as
a vehicle to bring into the world an evil created and stored in a
jar by the gods.[10]

Here, as in Virgil, similar descriptions occur which, while not
traceable to any source and perhaps original, are used in two
poems of different subject, for different purposes. Nonetheless,
each shows a similar conception, one might say mentality, behind
it. There is nothing like this in Homer.

Repetitions from one work to another of Homer's are of two
chief kinds: repeated short formulas, which are not relevant to
this study, and the less frequent repeated descriptions and similes,
which are.[11] A comparison of Homer's two poems shows a reluctance

---

[10] Οὕτως οὔτι πη ἔστι Διὸς νόον ἐξαλέασθαι. (*Works* 105) Ὣς οὐκ ἔστι Διὸς
κλέψαι νόον οὐδὲ παρελθεῖν. (*Theogony* 613). See P. P. Matsen, *Hesiod's Works
and Days and Homeric Oral Poetry*, Dissertation, Bryn Mawr, 1969, 64.

[11] Some of Homer's repeated verses can be significant beyond the limits
of the arguments concerning the formula. The two prayers of Chryses that
are repeated in *Il.* 1.37 and 451 use the same invocation to Apollo for effect.
Thetis refers to the correspondence between *Il.* 11.357ff. and 18.35ff. in 17.74.

to repeat significant passages. One reason for this is that the most important descriptions and similes in the *Iliad* occur in battle-scenes, of which there are many fewer in the *Odyssey*. The formulaic elements are of course present in both poems; the same gods and men are referred to by the same noun-epithet combinations and rosy dawn still leaves her saffron couch at daybreak. Repeated similes, however, are rare. Of the 241 objects of comparison used for similes in the *Iliad* and *Odyssey*, only 27 are shared by both poems. Sixteen of these pertain to the natural world (out of 123 in both) and 11 are drawn from human activities (out of 118). In addition, it is difficult to find the kind of studied variation that we found in Hesiod or the thematic unity of Virgil, apart from stylistic differences that may affect the dating of the poems.

In short, while the formula or cliché may exist in high frequency in both poems, longer descriptions and similes are repeated more often within a single poem than from one to the other. Only 10% of the objects of comparison in the similes are shared by the two poems.

Even the tragedians provide little such repetition despite the restricted number of myths suitable for tragedy and the susceptibility of their texts to corruption. Many of the repetitions in Euripides have, like Virgil's, been considered interpolations.[12] We might

---

Under the heading of dramatic foreshadowing, we may put Hector's challenge to single combat in 7.77, anticipating the duel to come. But Homer is also careful not to repeat as when Helen names the principal heroes Agamemnon, Odysseus, Ajax and Idomeneus, omitting Diomedes who will figure prominently in the later books. He is not mentioned until the fourth book, culminating the review of Agamemnon's forces. On the other hand, Andromache, in her laments (*Il.* 22.447, 24.725), never mentions her future because this has been done by Hector at 6.450. K. Reinhardt, "Der Schild der Achilles", *Freundesgabe für E. R. Curtius*, Berne, 1956, 67, points out that the absence of a contest on the shield of Achilles shows Homer's un-willingness to anticipate the funeral games of *Il.* 23. For repeated descriptions, see W. Arend, "Die typischen Szenen bei Homer", *Problemata* 7 (1933), for battle-scenes, G. Strassburger, *Die kleinen Kämpfer der Ilias*, Dissertation, Frankfurt, 1954 and W. H. Friederich, "Verwundung und Tod in der Ilias", *Abh. Ak. Gött. Phil.-Hist.* 3 (1956).

[12] D. Page, *Actors Interpolations*, Oxford, 1934, A. Böckh, *Graecae Tragoediae Principium* Heidelburg, 1808, 241ff. Repetitions in comedy, on the other hand, seem deliberate, as *Clouds* 225 and 1503, used for humorous effect. See A. Meineke, *Fragmenta Comicorum Graecorum*, Berlin, 1970, I, 358-359 and for Aristophanes, Menander and Philemon especially, see S. Kann, *De Iteratis apud Poetas Antiquae et Mediae Comoediae Atticae*, Gissen, 1909. On Aristophanes, see H. W. Miller, "Repetition of Lines in Aristophanes" *AJP* 65 (1944), 26-36.

legitimately expect repetition in the *Troades* and the *Hecuba*, written ten years apart: Both deal with the fall of Troy, both are centered on Hecuba and a rather loosely connected series of events that revolves around her. But Euripides manifestly refuses to repeat not only the most powerful scenes from the first play to the second, but indeed any sections of scenes. For instance, the death of Polyxena is simply mentioned in five lines of the *Troades* (39-40, 618-620), whereas in the earlier play it had occupied the bulk of the action. Two of the principal characters of the *Hecuba*, Polydorus and Polymestor, are not even mentioned in the later play. Indeed, the most extensive genuine repetition in Euripides is only one verse long: [13]

ἄλλως δ' ἐμόχθουν καὶ κατεξάνθην πόνοις

*Medea* 1030

μάτην δ' ἐμόχθουν καὶ κατεξάνθην πόνοις.

*Troades* 760

In short, self-repetition is not a significant literary device in the writings before Virgil's time. However, when a writer chooses to treat either a highly complex topic in one work or two similar subjects in as many works, he is bound to repeat himself to some degree. Incidental repetitions, coincidences of diction, re-use of formulas or clichés, will always recur as long as men communicate. They are as frequent in poetry and high prose and as common to writing and speaking as they are to music and painting. What is unusual is the extreme reluctance to repeat sections of more than a line or sentence length from one work to another. In this regard, Virgil stands apart from these representative authors in both the size and number of his repetitions, and thus marks a departure from previous literary practice.

### SCHOLARSHIP ON REPETITIONS

There has been an abundance of criticism spent on Virgil's *Pastorals* and *Aeneids* [sic], but the *Georgics* are a subject which none of the critics have sufficiently taken into their consideration, most of them passing it over in silence, or casting it under the same head with *Pastoral*—a division by no means proper, unless we suppose the style of a Husbandman ought to be limited in a

---

[13] Cook, 258-259, adduces 24 verbal parallels between the two plays, of which this is the longest.

> *Georgic*, as that of a shepherd is in the *Pastoral*...
> the precepts of husbandry are not to be delivered with
> the simplicity of a Plowman, but with the address of a
> Poet.[14]

So wrote John Addison in 1697 of the neglect and confusion surrounding the poem that Montaigne over 100 years earlier had called "le plus accomply ouvrage de la Poësie" and which Robert Burns nearly 100 years after Addison would call "by far the best of Virgil." [15] But until recent years, the Virgilian scholar might well have echoed Addison's plaint. Until 1964, Sellar had given the only full treatment of the *Georgics* as a literary work,[16] and his voice remained alone before the publication of Otis' book.[17]

The *Georgics* has for so long failed to receive its due as a literary work that it has not yet been thoroughly considered as a literary and stylistic predecessor of the *Aeneid*. Yet this it must be if only for the numerous major repetitions of material from the earlier work to the later. But Virgilians have failed as a rule to deal with this aspect of the matter. The authenticity of the text, the authorship of the *Appendix Vergiliana*, the order of composition of the poems, and other such unsolvable argumentative pastimes have been the chief interests of those who dealt with repetition. While allusions to other authors have been catalogued and discussed, the conclusions drawn from such work have not been applied to the problem of *self*-quotation.

Yet, as we have seen, Virgil's repetitions are unique; they seem to have no identifiable ancestry. Some critics, as I shall show, have tried to link this fact with the equally unparalleled half-lines. But it is rather because of the essential similarities between two poems of different genres that such repetition could take place. If no other poet repeated in this manner, it is due not only to his not writing two poems of different genre, but also to the fact that few authors were capable of transforming one genre by the language of another, as Virgil transformed didactic by the infusion of epic language and similes.

---

[14] John Addison, "Essay on the *Georgics*", *The Works of Addison*, ed. J. Hurd, London, 1862, 154. The essay was anonymously appended to the translation of Dryden who, it will be remembered, called the *Georgics* "the best poem by the best poet."

[15] Montaigne, *Essais*, II, 10; Burns, Letter to Mrs. Dunlop, May 4, 1788.

[16] W. Y. Sellar, *The Roman Poets of the Augustan Age: Virgil*, Oxford, 1877, 174-276.

[17] Otis, 144-214. See Wilkinson, 1-3, 314-315 for a survey of the scholarship.

The starting point for any understanding of this matter is the following passage from the *Vita Donati*:

> Aeneida prosa prius oratione formatam digestamque in XII libros particulatim componere instituit, prout liberet quidque, et nihil in ordinem arripiens. Ac ne quid impetum moraretur, quaedam inperfecta transmisit, alia levissimus versibus veluti fulsit, quae per iocum pro tibicinibus interponi aiebat ad sustinendum opus, donec solidae columnae advenirent.[18]

In other words, Virgil, working on random gobbets of his poem, would insert either half-lines (*inperfectus*) or trivial lines (*levissimus*) in order to finish the passage at hand (*ad sustinendum opus*). These temporary lines, which he intended either to excise or improve, were called *tibicines*.

Servius and Macrobius both characterize Virgil's practice of *repetitio* as a slight alteration of lines rather than an exact repetition.[19] Modern scholarship has not, until recent years, improved on the statements of the ancients: All concentrate on individual repeated lines (as opposed to extended passages) and none assembles all the evidence.

E. Albrecht gathers the repetitions into groups which he labels "mehr oder minder formelhaft", "absichtliche Wiederholungen," "nothdurftige vorlaufige Lückenbusser" (stopgaps), and those that are imitative of Homer.[20] He concludes that since he cannot find lines repeated within any one book of the *Aeneid*, that the poem was composed one book at a time, with the repetitions caused by lapses in the poet's memory. He mistakenly differentiates between exactly and nearly repeated lines. Since exact or unvaried repetitions are few, he concludes that Virgil altered a word here and there simply to avoid word-for-word repetition.

F. Gladow attempts to prove the authenticity of the *Appendix Vergiliana* on the basis of the repeated lines and phrases.[21] Like

---

[18] *Vita Donati*, 23-24.

[19] Servius, *ad Aen.* 9.814, has been taken by Heinsius and Forbiger as evidence that ancient critics agreed that Virgil usually altered a line when he repeated it. (J. Sparrow, *Half-Lines and Repetitions in Virgil*, Oxford, 1931, 24). Macrobius, *Sat.* 3.5.8 cites ten of Virgil's repetitions and comments on *repetitio* as a device.

[20] E. Albrecht, "Wiederholte Verse und Versteile bei Virgil", *Hermes* 16 (1881), 393-444.

[21] F. Gladow, *De Vergilio ipsius imitatore*, Dissertation Greifswald, 1921.

Albrecht, Gladow does not compile all the repetitions, and makes no distinction between repeated units of different lengths.[22]

The only book on the subject is J. Sparrow's *Half-Lines and Repetitions in Virgil*.[23] The book uses the passage from the *Vita* quoted above as a basis for considering the half-lines and repetitions as evidence for the incompleteness of the *Aeneid*. Sparrow concludes that interpolation is frequent in the text of Virgil and that "it is almost certain that many repetitions are the result of the incompleteness of the poem." [24] It must be remembered that Sparrow, like the others mentioned, is primarily concerned with the repetition of individual lines and phrases. Of the longer repetitions he says, "On practically every occasion where the repetition is more than two lines long, the original passage occurred in the *Georgics*; these repetitions are accompanied by no marks of incompleteness, and they must have been deliberate. This fact suggests very strongly that Virgil thought repetition of one poem in another in certain circumstances permissable, but avoided self-repetition [extended self-quotation within a single poem]." [25]

What may be called the current renaissance in scholarship on the *Georgics* began around 1964, with Otis' close comparison of the stylistic factors in *Georgics* 4 and *Aeneid* 1 that relate to the chronology of their composition.[26] There have since been several studies of themes and passages common to the two poems.[27] But as yet

---

[22] J. Perret, *Virgile, l'homme et l'oeuvre*, Paris, 1967, 185, calls the work "incomplet, mais commode." Other studies of the subject include F.X.-J. Roiron, *Étude sur l'imagination auditive de Virgile*, Paris, 1909, a study of repeated sound patterns, termed "hantises verbales" (esp. the word *sonus*), V. Henselmann, *Die Widerspruche in Vergils Aeneis*, Würzburg, 1914, an account of different descriptions of similar events in the *Aeneid*, N. Moseley, "The Repeated Lines of Virgil", *TAPA* 52 (1922), xx, an abstract that has not, to my knowledge, been published in final form, and two dissertations, F. L. Newton, *Studies in Verbal Repetition in Virgil*, Dissertation North Carolina, Chapel Hill, 1953, a study of words and phrases repeated in proximity in the *Aeneid*, and W. Moskalew, *Verbal Repetition in Vergil's Aeneid*, Dissertation Yale, New Haven, 1975, which works along similar lines.

[23] See n. 19 for full citation.

[24] Sparrow, 1.

[25] Ibid., 111.

[26] Otis, 408-413. For an opposite view, see K. Mylius, *Die wiederholten Verse bei Virgil*, Dissertation Freiburg, 1946, which had great influence on Büchner and Richter who feel that the ending of the fourth *Georgic* as we have it was composed or finished after Virgil had started on *Aeneid* 1.

[27] Most will be found in the Bibliography. The listings there may not accurately reflect the lack of scholarship on this matter. For instance, Wilkinson barely notes parallels with the *Aeneid* (157, 199-200, 203n, 217n)

there is no examination of the similes in the *Aeneid* that draw directly on passages in the *Georgics*. No one has compared the repeated elements to similar elements in Virgil's sources to determine exactly what is Virgilian in these passages and what is not. Conclusions on *what* is Virgilian may inspire others to speculate on *why* it is Virgilian. That is not my purpose here. Nor shall I treat frequencies of metrical figures, political ideas, religion, or philosophy as they are reflected in both poems. Instead, I shall examine the relevant passages in both poems, trying to extract the definitely Virgilian from the conventional. This done, I shall hope to have shown that not only stylistic features, but even Virgil's conception of nature in the *Georgics*, not only inform crucial elements of the *Aeneid* but are essential in the transformation of the didactic poem beyond the conventional limits of the genre.

---

and discusses the Aristaeus Epyllion without reference to the *Aeneid* at all (108-120). C. Hardie calls the *Georgics* "a transitional poem" ("The *Georgics*: A Transitional Poem", *Third Jackson Knight Memorial Lecture*, Berkshire, 1971), but only as it develops from the *Eclogues*, not into the *Aeneid*. An extreme example of misunderstanding the nature of these repetitions is given by E. Coleiro, "Allegory in the IVth Georgic", *Vergiliana: Recherches sur Virgile*, ed. H. Bardon & R. Verdière, Leiden, 1971, 121, "after finishing the *Georgics*, [Virgil] began the *Aeneid* writing only book I, II and IV... without repeating himself at all and then, on compulsion, he changed the end of the IVth Georgic...and that then, having finished them [*Aen.* 1, 2, 4] as quickly as he could, he proceeded with the *Aeneid* to his heart's content, full of his epic inspiration, and, consequently, *never repeating himself again* (italics mine). It is the aim of this study to disprove statements like this one.

CHAPTER ONE

# SIMILES IN THE *GEORGICS*
## USED FOR
# SIMILES IN THE *AENEID*

Even before the *Aeneid* was conceived, Virgil was adapting the language of previous epic for the *Georgics*. At the same time, he was adapting from a variety of sources similes and descriptive passages which, once altered to fit the didactic, would reappear in the *Aeneid*, changed again. By examining such repeated passages and the changes made in each occurrence, I hope to show how much of Virgil's epic technique saw its first use in the *Georgics*. For Virgil's similes in a sense depend upon the changes he made in Homeric or Apollonian material, not only by the combination or contrast of elements from two or three sources, but by the unique alterations of his received material that accommodate the simile to his stylistic as well as narrative needs.

Homer established the predominance of comparisons to nature in epic similes, especially in the *Iliad* where nature similes are more numerous than in the *Odyssey*[1] and occur primarily in battle scenes.[2] For all their artistic beauty and functional importance, the similes of Homer, like his narration, illustrate the crucial fact of his style, namely his "objectivity."[3] That is, the comparee of the simile usually resembles the comparand in the most superficial way. When Hector and Patroclus fight in *Il.* 16.823-826, they are

---

[1] No exact or canonic number of similes in the Homeric poems can be arrived at or agreed upon. Each scholar who compiles a catalogue has a larger number of entries than the last. The most recent compilation available to me is that of D. J. N. Lee, *The Similes of the Iliad and Odyssey Compared*, Melbourne, 1964. Using his statistics, I find that in the similes of the *Iliad* there are 318 subjects of comparison drawn from the natural world and of the 132 similes of the *Odyssey*, the corresponding figure is 57. These numbers are slightly artificial in that they do not allow for double or triple subjects within a single simile. At any rate, it is the proportion that is important rather than the exact totals.

[2] C. M. Bowra, *Tradition and Design in the Iliad*, Oxford, 1930, 117, finds 164 battle scenes in the *Iliad* that contain similes, "because fighting scenes tend to become monotonous and therefore need variation".

[3] On the difference between Homer's "objectivity" and Virgil's "subjectivity", see Heinze, 370-371 and Otis, 61-62.

compared to a lion and a boar fighting over a small spring. The comparison is one of size and strength with only the barest motivational or psychological detail. The motivation is explained in Hector's speech preceding the duel (830-842), not in the simile itself. The separation of the causes of the act from the description of the act itself limits the depth of Homeric similes. As Heinze and Otis have shown in detail, Virgil's "subjective style" is radically different.

The nature similes of Apollonius deal more with heavenly phenomena than with the terrestial, possibly due to the popularity of astronomy in Alexandria. While his similes as a whole use many points of comparison found in Homer, one-third of them do not.[4] Apollonius also uses his similes to reflect narrative events more directly than do the more spontaneous similes of Homer, and he employs fewer similes for each object of comparison.

The most important point about Apollonius' similes, however, is that first made by Schadewaldt, namely that following the immensely popular "psychological" dramas of Euripides and writing in an Alexandria that favored the personal and reflective in literature rather than the heroic and descriptive, Apollonius was the first to use the simile to express an emotion other than rage or fear.[5] The psychological depiction which had been only elementary in Homer is developed for an audience that could not accept the simplistic motivation of Homer's characters any more than it could his gods and heroes.

Few fragments of early Latin poetry can be identified as similes,[6] and so we can say little about the similes of writers from Ennius to Catullus. Catullus gives Virgil some similes,[7] but other influences are more difficult to detect. The greatest influence of Lucretius upon Virgil's style is apparent not in the quotations of similes and descriptions but rather in the crucial placement and function of Virgil's similes within the structure of the entire poem, be it the *Georgics* or the *Aeneid*.[8] As the following chart shows, there are

---

[4] E. G. Wilkins, "A Classification of the Similes in the *Argonautica* of Apollonius Rhodius", *CW* 14 (1921), 162-166 gives exact figures.

[5] W. Schadewaldt, *Iliasstudien*, *ASAW*, 43, 6, Leipzig, 1938, 120-124.

[6] Wigodsky (132-139) lists only those similes that can be traced in Virgil's work and they are primarily from Lucretius. Only one (*Geo.* 1.512-514) is from Ennius (60).

[7] *Aen.* 9.436-437 from Cat. 11.22-24 and Sappho 105cL-P.

[8] B. Otis, "Virgilian Narrative in the Light of Its Precursors and Successors" *SPh* 73 (1976), 15-23.

echoes of Lucretius in seven of the repeated similes, but they are generally details added to an already predominantly Homeric or Apollonian simile.

As there has been no full study of the similes in the *Georgics*, I shall list the 29 similes I have found, arranged in the order of their occurrence.[9] An asterisk denotes a simile drawn from nature. "H" refers to a similar object of comparison in Homer, "A" to one in Apollonius.

## SIMILES IN THE *GEORGICS*

| | Sources | Subject |
|---|---|---|
| Geo. I | | |
| 201-203 | Hesiod | Man like one rowing skiff |
| *245 | Aratus | Snake glides like river |
| 303-304 | Aratus | Farmers like sailors |
| 512-514 | H, Ennius | Mars like charioteer |
| Geo. II | | |
| *105-106 | H, A | Number of vines like grains of sand |
| *107-108 | Catullus | Number of vines like waves |
| 250 | Lucr. (?) | Soil like pitch |
| 279-283 | Lucr., Varro | Agriculture like battle |
| Geo. III | | |
| * 99-100 | H, A | Old horse like fire |
| 193 | | Horse like man working hard |
| *196-198 | H | Horse like winds |
| *237-241 | H | Bull like wave |
| *239 | Lucr. | Wave like mountain |
| 346-348 | Lucr., Varro | African shepherd like Roman soldier |
| *470-471 | H, A | Plague like whirlwind |
| Geo. IV | | |
| * 80 | H, A | Bees like hail |
| * 81 | H. | Bees like acorns |
| 95 | Callimachus | Bees like traveller |
| 170-175 | H, Hesiod, Call; | Bees like Cyclops |
| 194-196 | | Bees like ships |
| *261 | H, A | Murmur of bees like South wind |
| *262 | H, Lucr. | Murmur of bees like sea |
| 263 | Lucr. | Murmur of bees like fire's hiss |
| *312-313 | | Bees like shower |
| 313-314 | A | Bees like arrow |
| 433-436 | H | Proteus like shepherd |
| *473-475 | Bacchylides, Soph. H | Shades like birds |
| *499-500 | H (Lucr.) | Eurydice like smoke |
| *511-514 | H, Aesch., Soph. | Orpheus like Nightingale |

[9] I have omitted as too brief the simple comparisons at *Geo.* 2.250, 3.522, 4.41, and also *Geo.* 2.131, the citron compared to the bay tree.

In general, the number of similes increases sharply between Book 1-2 and 3-4. Thus, Book 4, the most epic of the *Georgics*, contains nearly half the similes of the entire poem (14). Similarly, the proportion of nature similes increases (3 of 8 in 1-2, 13 of 21 in 3-4). Sixteen of the similes recall epic or tragedy with Homer being the most common source (12). Unlike comparisons of men or gods to natural phenomena in Homer or the *Aeneid*, the similes of the *Georgics*, in accordance with their subject-matter, most often compare one thing in nature with another (18). One interesting stylistic difference between these similes and those of the *Aeneid* is that while 71 of the 79 extended similes in the *Aeneid* have the same word used in both the narrative and simile parts of the simile, only 6 of the 20 extended similes in the *Georgics* have such a correspondence.[10]

The most important point about these similes is that they occur in didactic at all. Virgil used these similes for three reasons: 1) past epic provided a ready store of nature similes that could be used or adapted either as similes or descriptions; 2) by recalling their epic milieu and tone, they could ennoble otherwise mundane expository passages; 3) some could be set at significant points in the poem, not merely to enhance the narration but to advance the action or clinch a passage with what Klingner called a *Schlussfigur*. These characteristics will appear in the course of the discussion.

Ten similes of the *Georgics* are echoed in the *Aeneid*.[11] Because of the relative rarity of similes in didactic, these comparisons are usually more significant in the *Georgics*.

One repetition is a short verbal reminiscence of the evaporation of Eurydice as Anchises' ghost disappears:

> Dixit et ex oculis subito, ceu fumus in auras
> commixtus tenuis, fugit diversa...
>
> > (*Geo.* 4.499-500)
>
> Dixerat et tenuis fugit ceu fumus in auras.
>
> > (*Aen.* 5.740)
>
> par levibus ventis volucrique simillima somno.
>
> > (*Aen.* 2.794 = 6.702)

---

[10] On the *Aeneid* similes, see J. Perkins, "An Aspect of Latin Comparison Construction", *TAPA*, 104 (1974), 267. The *Georgics* similes that *do* show verbal parallels are 1.196-198, 3.470-471, 4.194-196, 433-436, 499-500, 511-515.

[11] I omit *Geo.* 3.239-240: *Aen.* 9.674 as too brief to be of consequence.

The comparison of death and disappearing smoke is seen in
*Il.* 23.99-101, where the shade of Patroclus goes to ground ἠΰτε
καπνός. The compression of two lines of the *Georgics* describing
smoke in the winds into one in the *Aeneid* (along with the change
of tense to *dixerat*) stresses the suddenness with which Anchises'
spirit vanishes rather than the utter evaporation of Eurydice.
C. P. Segal finds that the words *ex oculis, subito,* and *diversa* all
"heighten the emotional tone" while the epic simile "as befits its
theme and its hero, is more austere than the epyllion." [12] In the
comparison to sleep and breezes in *Aeneid* 2 and 6, Virgil stresses
the unreality and ambiguity of the situation at Troy by using two
generalized comparands.

Another stock simile compares the number of waves on a stormy
sea:

> quem qui scire velit, Libyci velit aequoris idem
> discere quam multae Zephyro turbentur harenae
> aut, ubi navigiis violentior incidit Eurus,
> nosse quot Ionii veniant ad litora fluctus.
>
> (*Geo.* 2.105-108)

> quam multi Libyco volvontur marmore fluctus
> saevos ubi Orion hibernis conditur undis,
> vel cum sole novo densae torrentur aristae
> aut Hermi campo aut Lyciae flaventibus arvis.
>
> (*Aen.* 7.718-721)

To *Il.* 2.144-148 (Agamemnon's address stirs the Greeks as the
wind raises sea-waves and disturbs the cornfield), Apollonius added
a comparison of numberless leaves at *Arg.* 4.214 to describe the
countless number of Colchians inflamed with love for Medea. For
the *Aeneid*, Virgil combines Homer's cornfield with Apollonius'
troops. He also joins the references to Libyan sand and Ionian
billows from the *Georgics* in the phrase *Libyco marmore*.[13]

A rather conventional simile of the effect of the whirlwind is
less structural than ornamental:

---

[12] C. P. Segal, " 'Like Winds and Winged Dream': A Note on Virgil's
Development", *CJ* 69 (1973-1974), 99. Segal also examines other examples
of vanishing souls, *Aen.* 4.704-705, 10.818-820, 11.615-617.
[13] Virgil adds *Libyci,* perhaps from Cat. 7.3 and 61.199-201. See also
Herod. 1.47 and Pind *Pyth.* 9.83ff. where these themes are joined. Richter
(199) feels the humorous element from Catullus is unsuited to the *Georgics*
passage. The comparison (without place-name) is also found in Theoc. 16.60.

Non tam creber agens hiemem ruit aequore turbo
quam multae pecudum pestes.

(*Geo.* 3.470-471)

adversi rupto ceu quondam turbine venti
confligunt, Zephyrusque Notusque et laetus Eois
Eurus equis; stridunt silvae saevitque tridenti
spumeus aque imo Nereus ciet aequora fundo.

(*Aen.* 2.416-419)

Magno discordes aethere venti
proelia ceu tollunt animis et viribus aequis;
non ipsi inter se, non nubila, non mare cedit;

(*Aen.* 10.356-358)

Talia per campos edebat funera ductor
Dardanius, torrentis aquae vel turbinis atri
more furens

(*Aen.* 10.602-604)

At vero ingentem quatiens Mezentius hastam
turbidus ingreditur campo.

(*Aen.* 10.762-763)

Haec effatus ecum in medios, moriturus et ipse,
concitat et Venulo adversum se turbidus infert...

(*Aen.* 11.741-742)

Volat atri turbinis instar
exitium dirum hasta ferens orasque recludit
loricae et clipei extremos septemplicis orbis

(*Aen.* 12.923-925)

In the *Georgics*, the disruption of the herd of cows by the plague is compared to the size and force of a whirlwind, with the visualization of the disturbance accentuated by the juxtaposition of "aequore," the level sea, and "turbo," the whirlwind. In *Aeneid* 2, the simile refers to the double attack on Aeneas, first by the weapons of his own men on the roofs, and then by the Greeks mustering on the ground. The comparison focuses on the opposition of the winds (*adversi*), rather than their strength. Other elements of this simile recall the description of the storm in *Geo.* 1.318ff. which I shall discuss later.

Later uses of this simile conventionally elaborate clashing forces in battle (10.357), Aeneas in battle (10.603-604), Mezentius in battle (10.763), and Tarchon (11.742), all much as in *Il.* 11.297-298 where Hector rushing onto the battlefield is described as a whirlwind in his might (also *Il.* 12.40, 13.39 and 23.366). These similes in the latter six books of the *Aeneid* are simpler comparisons than those in *Georgics* 3 and *Aeneid* 2, a characteristic we shall see again. But in two of them, the objective *turbo*, the comparand, is replaced by *turbidus*, which describes a man and reinforces the notion of emotional struggle within his character.

The remaining example of this simile is its comparison to the spear with which Aeneas wounds Turnus in Book 12. Again it is the force of the wind that is compared.

Saepe ego, cum flavis messorem induceret arvis
agricola et fragili iam stringeret hordea culmo,
omnia ventorum concurrere proelia vidi,...
                    ...ruit arduus aether,
et pluvia ingenti sata laeta boumque labores
diluit; implentur fossae et cava flumina crescunt...

*(Geo.* 1.316-326)

Frigidus in Venerem senior frustraque laborem
ingratum trahit et, si quando ad proelia ventumst,
ut quondam in stipulis magnus sine viribus ignis,
in cassum furit.

*(Geo.* 3.97-100)

in segetem veluti cum flamma furentibus Austris
incidit aut rapidus montano flumine torrens
sternit agros, sternit sata laeta bovumque labores,
praecipitisque trahit silvas; stupet inscius alto
accipiens sonitum saxi de vertice pastor.

*(Aen.* 2.304-308)

Ac velut immissi diversis partibus ignes
arentem in silvam et virgulta sonantia lauro,
aut ubi decursu rapido de montibus altis
dant sonitum spumosi amnes et in aequora currunt
quisque suum populatus iter: non segnius ambo
Aeneas Turnusque ruunt per proelia; nunc, nunc
fluctuat ira intus, rumpuntur nescia vinci
pectora, nunc totis in volnera viribus itur.

*(Aen.* 12.521-528)

The passage describing the sudden storm in *Georgics* 1 influences the other three passages, although it is not a simile.

In *Geo.* 3.72-94, Virgil gives a highly empathetic description of an old sire-horse: the proud leader of the herd becomes almost human in his inability to ignore the distant clash of arms. His comparison to legendary war-horses is concluded by a reference to

Saturn who turned himself into a horse to avoid his jealous wife. The distinction between horse and man is therefore eliminated in the climax of this passage, after which Virgil describes the horse now sick and old by a simile which could, out of context, apply to a man as well as a horse. The final incarceration of the horse by his owner is made all the more poignant because, having been described in human terms, the horse is, in the end, not treated humanely.

The basic simile comes from Homer's comparisons of growing anger of men and animals to a mountain fire.[14] But Virgil reverses the precedent by using the simile to show the *flagging* of the horse's power.

In *Aeneid* 2, two passages from the *Georgics* form one that is unlike any of its models. The Greeks are like a flame fanned by the South Wind, or the current of a mountain stream, both of which raze fields, farms and forests. Besides these elements, Virgil adds a subjective element; Aeneas inserts himself into the simile, comparing himself to an *inscius pastor*, much as Virgil describes himself watching the destruction of land and crops in *Geo.* 1.316-321. The repetition of *sternit* in *Aen.* 1.306 and the use of *stupet* in 307 underscore Aeneas' reaction to the tragedy. From the storm scene in the *Georgics* come the words *sata laeta boumque labores*,[15] *laeta* having the subjective meaning "happy" as well as "rich," and *boum* used where one might have expected *hominum*.

The significant point, however, is that the unique elements of this simile come from the *Georgics* and no other source. These subjective elements do not occur in the later uses in the *Aeneid*.

In Book 12, Aeneas and Turnus, fighting side by side, are compared by similes linking Homer's mountain fire and Apollonius' brushfire.[16] Aeneas is now an agent of destruction, and both he and Turnus are deliberately pursuing their ends. The simile echoes the fire-simile in Book 10 where the shepherd Pallas inflames his men [17] and that in *Iliad* 11 where Athena rouses the Greeks to battle.

---

[14] The chief model here is the description of the waves and fire at *Il.* 14.394-401 (see also 11.155-162, 15.605-606, 20.490-494). Apollonius, 1.1027, uses the comparison both for the Argonauts and for the Doliones.

[15] Cicero notes that *laetas segetes* is an old rustic phrase (*De Orat.* 3.38.135).

[16] The crackling sound of the brushfire perhaps comes from Lucretius' simile of the thunder at 6.152-155.

[17] The torrents flow over fields to the sea in *Il.* 16.391 but they flow to the plain in 11.492. Virgil uses the word *aequore* which can mean either "plain" or "sea". See W. W. Fowler, *The Death of Turnus*, Oxford, 1919, 106.

In short, the *Georgics* simile occurs in a context opposite to Homer's; the simile in *Aeneid* 2 combines the Homeric context with the viewpoint of another scene from the *Georgics*; the simile in *Aeneid* 12 is more Homeric in its relatively objective description of the two raging warriors.

Virgil also humanizes bulls:

> Post, ubi collectum robur viresque refectae,
> signa movet praecepsque oblitum fertur in hostem,
> fluctus uti, medio coepit cum albescere ponto,
> longius ex altoque sinum trahit utque volutus
> ad terras immane sonat per saxa neque ipso
> monte minor procumbit; at ima exaestuat unda
> verticibus nigramque alte subiectat harenam.
>
> *(Geo.* 3.235-241)

> atraque late
> horrescit strictis seges ensibus aeraque fulgent
> sole lacessita et lucem sub nubila iactant:
> fluctus uti primo coepit cum albescere vento,
> paulatim sese tollit mare et altius undas
> erigit, inde imo consurgit ad aethera fundo.
>
> *(Aen.* 7.525-530)

In the *Georgics*, the simile is a *Schlussfigur*, ending the discussion of love among cattle and horses and preparing for the peroration on love in general.[18] Like the horse, the bull, who has lost a heifer to a rival, is humanized. An exile, he has prepared himself for a rematch and is victorious with his new-found strength.

The model seems to be *Il.* 4.422-428,[19] in which the movement of the Greek ranks into battle is like the swell of the sea waves, gradually gathering momentum until the billows break on the shore and spew forth the salty brine. *Sonat per saxa* may come from αἰγιαλῷ πολυηχέϊ (the sounding beach) and the foaming brine becomes tossed-up black sand.

Virgil also adds the aftermath of the wave, the simile-within-a-simile, *(neque ipso/monte minor),* and the visual aspect, absent in Homer, of the whitening sea *(albescere).* This element as well as *subiectat harenam* may recall Lucretius.[20] Whether or not, the

---

[18] See below, pp. 46.

[19] See also Soph. *Ant.* 586-591.

[20] For the whitening sea, see Lucr. 2.766-767. For *subiectat harenam*, see 6.700, the description of Aetna, with the sea breaking and then backwashing *(saxaque subiectare et harenae tollere nimbos).* There is also perhaps a reminiscence of Cat. 64.270-273.

additions portray: 1) the new power of the bull, as the sea whitens
in its growing strength; 2) the effect of that power, crashing against
its foe (at the hephthemimeral caesura in 240); 3) and the struggles
of the defeated bull kicking up black (bloody?) sand.

The comparee is changed from Homer and the *Georgics* for the
*Aeneid*, as the battle of the Trojan and Latin youths is compared
to a sea roused by the wind. Again, the simile is largely visual,
emphasizing the change of appearance of the youths once they have
been enflamed by battle. Virgil also adds the "crop of swords"
description from *Geo.* 2.142. Here the influence of Lucretius con-
tributes to the central point: Virgil's wheat-fields had bristled
with glistening spears that refracted the sunlight. Now suddenly
the wheat-field is changed from a peaceful place to a battleground,
just as the sea is transformed from placid to raging.

The first line of each simile is identical, but in the *Aeneid* the
result, the breaking of the wave, is absent from the simile because
Virgil will describe the battle directly in the lines to come. Both
stress the appearance of the wave, but the *Aeneid* adds the per-
spective of the distant onlooker, rather like the *inscius pastor* of
*Aen.* 2.304-308. The simile in the *Georgics* ends an important section,
not only illuminating but narrating the action. The other simile
advances the narrative by description in an epic manner, with
elements from Lucretius, to set the scene for the ensuing battle.

> concurritur aethere in alto
> fit sonitus, magnum mixtae glomerantur in orbem
> praecipitesque cadunt; non densior aëre grando
> nec de concussa tantum pluit ilice glandis.
>
> (*Geo.* 4.78-81)

> Nec mora nec requies: quam multa grandine nimbi
> culminibus crepitant, sic densis ictibus heros
> creber utraque manu pulsat versatque Dareta.
>
> (*Aen.* 5.458-460)

> verberat imber humum, quam multa grandine nimbi
> in vada praecipitant, cum Iuppiter horridus Austris
> torquet aquosam hiemem et caelo cava nubila rumpit.
>
> (*Aen.* 9.669-671)

The simile in the *Georgics* describes the bees in battle. As so
often in the mock-heroic descriptions of bee-life, the tone is height-
ened by reference to earlier epic. In this case the echo is from
Apollonius, *Arg.* 2.1083-1089 (the din of the birds' attack on the

heroes is like a hail-storm endured by people sitting quietly beneath their roofs) rather than Homer (e.g. *Il.* 15.170-172, Iris travels to earth like snow or acorns). Virgil keeps the tone partially light by comparing small things (hail & acorns) to small things (bees).

In *Aeneid* 5, he trades the light for the serious as he describes Entellus' punches falling upon Dares as thick as hail. The double simile becomes one, with the "c" and "s" sounds carried over (especially in 459), but with the expression of the comparison changed from a comparative adjective to a variation of the standard *quam...tam* coordination. Again the comparison involves the density of the attacking members, but Virgil adds persistence (*nec mora nec requies*) and stresses the din more directly (*culminibus crepitant*) than in the previous simile (*fit sonitus*).

The simile in Book 9 occurs in a double simile, like that of the *Georgics*, describing the clash of armies.[21] The central statement of the simile (669-670) quotes both 5.458 (*quam multa grandine nimbi*) and recalls *Geo.* 4.80 (*praecipitesque cadunt* becomes *praecipitant*). The changes produce not only a more concise statement but an effective allusion to the two previous similes that is surely deliberate.

> tum sonus auditur gravior tractimque susurrant,
> frigidus ut quondam silvis immurmurat Auster,
> ut mare sollicitum stridit refluentibus undis,
> aestuat ut clausis rapidus fornacibus ignis:
>
> (*Geo.* 4.260-263)

> Talibus orabat Iuno cunctique fremebant
> caelicolae adsensu vario, ceu flamina prima
> cum deprensa fremunt silvis et caeca volutant
> murmura venturos nautis prodentia ventos.
>
> (*Aen.* 10.96-99)

The bees are again described, this time with three similes in a row, as they make their mournful funeral procession. The emphasis here is on sound, as Richter says, for the lines have "eine intensive akustische Vorstellung" [22] with alliteration, end rhymes, and interior rhymes. The tone is mock-tragic, soon to be resolved in the next

---

[21] "The duplicating of similes in parallel sentences or clauses was employed by several Augustan poets as a means of stressing the importance of the passage by adding to its stylistic weight". E. Fraenkel, *Horace*, Oxford, 1957, 427. Other double similes in the *Aeneid* occur at 2.304-308, 4.469-473, 12.521-525.

[22] Richter, 368.

two lines (264-265) when men burn incense to lift the spirits of the bees.

Homer uses a triad of similes to describe the din of clashing armies at *Il.* 14.394-400. Lucretius at 6.142-155 describes three types of clouds that create a thunder. The thunder is then compared to breaking waves, white-hot iron, and a burning laurel. The basic simile in the *Georgics* is from Homer, with comparisons to wind in the trees, splashing waves, and the forest fire, but in a different order. Lucretius may have provided a verbal nuance. The important point is that Virgil's three majestic similes amplify the growing grief of the bees with a carefully balanced structure: each simile is one line long and is set off by the anaphora of *ut... ut... ut.*

This balance is lacking in the *Aeneid* simile which is more conventionally used. After Juno's speech, the murmuring of the *concilium deorum* is compared with the noise of wind in the trees. It not only shows the contrary forces at work in the council (*adsensu vario*) as well as the choice they find themselves forced to make (between one god and another), but also the *coming* storm, not the storm itself.[23] As we have already seen in other examples, the simile in the *Georgics* is far more significant than that in the *Aeneid*.

(modis animalia miris)...ut nervo pulsante sagittae,
prima leves ineunt si quando proelia Parthi.

*(Geo.* 4.313-314)

illa (navis) Noto citius volucrique sagitta
ad terram fugit et portu se condidit alto.

*(Aen.* 5.242-243)

fugit illa per undas
ocior et iaculo et ventos aequante sagitta;

*(Aen.* 10.247-248)

Non secus ac nervo per urbem inpulsa sagitta,
armatam saevi Parthus quam felle veneni,
Parthus sive Cydon, telum inmedicabile, torsit,
stridens et celeris incognita transilit umbras:
talis se sata Nocte tulit terrasque petivit.

*(Aen.* 12.856-860)

The first of these similes compares the bees born from *bugonia* to an arrow flying from a Parthian bow as a battle begins. It ends the formal section on bee-lore not with a dramatic *Schlussfigur* but

---

[23] R. A. Hornsby, *Patterns of Action in the Aeneid*, Iowa City, 1970, 34.

rather with a charming simile that enhances the military aspect of bee-life by comparing their beginning lives to the arrows which begin a battle. The emphasis seems to be (it is not explicit) on the hail of arrows which is as dense as a pack of bees.

*Aen.* 5.242-243 describe the ship sped on by Portunus' hand. It is an effective picture, comparing two things propelled by man's hand, but it is little more than a periphrasis, like Cymodocea's push in *Aen.* 10.248.

In Book 12, a Fury is sent by Jupiter from above and the simile from *Georgics* 4 is recalled. As in Book 5, Virgil emphasizes speed (*celerem*-853, *celerique*-855, *celeris*-859), reflecting a model, Apollonius 2.600, where Athena, having helped the Argonauts negotiate the clashing rocks at Pontus, speeds to Olympus like an arrow. Like Apollonius, Virgil compares one person (the Fury) to one arrow. He retains from the *Georgics* the Parthian element [24] and the echo of *nervo pulsante sagittae* in *nervo...impulsa sagitta.*

> At cantu commotae Erebi de sedibus imis
> umbrae ibant tenuis simulacraque luce carentum,
> quam multa in foliis avium se millia condunt,
> Vesper ubi aut hibernus agit de montibus imber,
>
> (*Geo.* 4.471-474)

> (huc omnis turba ad ripas effusa, ruebat:)
> quam multa in silvis autumni frigore primo
> lapsa cadunt folia, aut ad terram gurgite ab alto
> quam multae glomerantur aves, ubi frigidus annus
> trans pontum fugat et terris immittit apricis.
>
> (*Aen.* 6.309-312)

Here a single simile in the *Georgics* is expanded to a double simile in the *Aeneid*. Both passages describe the souls of the dead waiting to cross the Styx.

The bird-simile in the *Georgics* suggests elements of *Il.* 3.4-5, in which the din of the Trojan forces is compared to the squawking of cranes, *Od.* 11.36-41, the description of the shades flocking to the sacrificial trench, and Soph. *OT* 174-177, where the multitude

---

[24] The Parthian element, if it matters at all, rather than emphasizing the beginning of life, as in the *Georgics*, stresses the beginning of the final conflict of Turnus and Aeneas. Also, instead of a rain of arrows, the Fury comes to earth like a single arrow. The Parthian element is probably no more than a localizing detail, an Alexandrian characteristic common in the *Georgics*. See M. Glass, *The Fusion of Stylistic Elements in Virgil's Georgics* (Ph. D. dissertation, Columbia University, New York, 1913), 11-12, 16.

of the dying are like migrating birds. The simile also has internal reference in that it recalls the cranes of *Geo.* 1.374-375, the crows of *Geo.* 1.412-413,[25] and the bees of 4.18-24, all descriptions of animals behaving *en masse*. The passage is balanced, with two lines of description and two lines of comparison. The opening spondees of 471-473 yield to quick dactyls that emphasize the rushing of the shades to hear Orpheus' beautiful music.

In the *Aeneid*, Virgil expands the bird-simile from two lines to two-and-one-half and develops the leaves (the nesting-place of the birds) into a one-and-one-half line independent simile. The first simile is predominately spondaic, the second, dactylic. The leaf-comparison may derive from *Il.* 6.145-149, the comparison of generations of mankind to leaves, also found in Bacch. *Epin.* 5.63ff. and Apoll. 4.216-219. *Quam multa* begins the leaf-simile as it had the *Georgics* bird-simile, but it is postponed in the *Aeneid* bird-simile. Now the homecoming of the birds has become an autumn exodus to avoid the cold season, as emphasized by the ending of lines 309 (*frigore primo*) [26] and 311 (*frigidus annus*). In the *Georgics*, Virgil describes the nesting and then gives the reason for it. In the *Aeneid* leaf-simile, he gives the reason (*frigore*) then the action (*cadunt*), then does the reverse in the bird-simile (*glomerantur...  frigidus annus*). As Otis points out, the nesting birds imply a rising from the depths of the Underworld (*de sedibus imis*) while the *Aeneid* similes stress descent (*lapsa cadunt, ad terram gurgite ab alto*).[27]

*Geo.* 4.475-477 are obviously carefully worked. In 475 *atque* is unelided, as rarely in Virgil,[28] 476 begins with the archaic genitive *magnanimum* (Homer's μεγάθυμος), but ends with the prosaic and touching *puellae*. *Ante ora parentum* is, for Virgil, the most tragic way to die.[29] These lines precede the *Georgics* simile, according to Otis, because they stress the movement of the dead, while they follow the *Aeneid* similes to stress the pathos of the shades.[30]

While Virgil has borrowed many lines from the Underworld scene in the *Odyssey* (cf. *Geo.* 4.475-477 and *Od.* 11.36-41), that

---

[25] Esp. 413, *inter se foliis strepitant, iuvat imbribus actis*.

[26] Austin, VI, 130. Cf. *Geo.* 2.321, *prima vel autumni sub frigore*.

[27] Otis, 411.

[28] There are 35 examples in the *Aeneid* (B. Axelson, *Unpoetische Wörter*, Lund, 1945, 84).

[29] Austin, I, 56.

[30] Otis, 412.

scene contains no simile, but rather gains its effect from the procession of pathetic figures. Similarly, the simile of *Il.* 6.145-149 compares the death of innumerable generations to the withering of leaves, while Virgil speaks of just one generation. There have been many attempts to show that Virgil drew these combined similes from other sources, including a lost *Herakleos Katabasis*,[31] but clearly the similarity of language, the development of the leaf image, only adumbrated in the *Georgics*, and the careful alteration of structure, eliminate the need for such speculation and show the *Georgics* to be the primary source of the simile in the *Aeneid*.

Many of the techniques we have seen in the preceding similes are observable in the final simile of *Geo.* 1.

> saevit toto Mars impius orbe,
> ut, cum carceribus sese effudere, quadrigae
> addunt in spatia et frustra retinacula tendens
> fertur equis auriga neque audit currus habenas.

> *(Geo.* 1.511-514)

> Infidunt pariter sulcos totumque dehiscit
> convolsum remis rostrisque tridentibus aequor.
> Non tam praecipites biiugo certamine campum
> corripuere ruuntque effusi carcere currus,
> nec sic immissis aurigae undantia lora
> concussere iugis pronique in verbera pendent.

> *(Aen.* 5.142-147)

Macrobius gives the source of this simile as *Od.* 13.81-83: [32]

ἡ δ᾽, ὥς τ᾽ ἐν πεδίῳ τετράοροι ἄρσενες ἵπποι,
πάντες ἅμ᾽ ὁρμηθέντες ὑπὸ πληγῇσιν ἱμάσθλης,
ὑψόσ᾽ ἀειρόμενοι ῥίμφα πρήσσουσι κέλευθον,

It is also clear that Virgil had in mind the description of the chariot-race in the games for Patroclus in *Il.* 23.362-370.[33]

---

[31] R. J. Clarke, "Two Virgilian Similes and the *Herakleos Katabasis*", *Phoenix* 24 (1970), 244-255, finds a clearer reference to Bacchylides in the position and subject of the simile of the leaves in the *Georgics*. R. Cahen, "Pour Virgile", *REG* 45 (1932), 1-6, describes the reduction, in these lines, of the *Nekuia* of *Od.* XI. H. Lloyd-Jones, "Heracles at Eleusis, P. Oxy. 2622 and P.S.I. 1391" *Maia* 19 (1967), 206-229, suggests that the papyrus in question is from Pindar and was used by Virgil for the leaf-simile. G. Thaniel, "Vergil's Leaf-and-Bird Similes of Ghosts", *Phoenix* 25 (1971), 237-245, disputes this and Clarke's position.

[32] *Sat.* 5.11.20.

[33] See also Aesch. *PV* 906, *Cho.* 161, Soph. *El.* 699.

The two Virgilian similes show different aspects of Virgil's borrowing. In the *Georgics*, unlike Homer or Apollonius, he compares a human activity to a state of mind, a political atmosphere. On the surface, the race is like the raging of Mars, much as human anger in Homer is like that of ravenous lions. But the *Georgics* simile, linked structurally with the simile of the uncontrollable *currus* at 202-203, describes pessimistically the political condition of man much as the previous simile had described the dour toil of the farmer.

Moreover, the simile ends the book with a climactic description of the political world falling apart for want of a *moderator*.[34]

There is another chariot-race in the *Georgics*:

> Nonne vides, cum praecipiti certamine campum
> corripuere ruuntque effusi carcere currus,
> cum spes arrectae iuvenum exsultantiaque haurit
> corda pavor pulsans? Illi instant verbere torto
> et proni dant lora; volat vi fervidus axis;
> iamque humiles iamque elati sublime videntur
> aëra per vacuum ferri atque adsurgere in auras.
> Nec mora nec requies; at fulvae nimbus harenae
> tollitur, umescunt spumis flatuque sequentum:
> tantus amor laudum, tantaest victoria curae.
>
> (*Geo.* 3.103-112)

Here, in a narrative passage, are all the familiar Virgilian effects that build a passage to a climax: alliteration, anaphora, varied cola lengths, alternating caesural patterns, a dactylic series of lines followed by a spondaic sequence, and so on. All of these effects build to the final *Ausklang*, the pointed theme of the passage in the last line and its balanced, almost liturgical clarity.

The picture is an expansion of the end of Book 1, but with a difference that is significant. Virgil adds to the Ennian echoes [35] the psychological state of the drivers in 105-106, with their *pavor* and *spes*. He stresses not just the action, but the emotion and motivation of the race. Ennius had already done this from the spectator's point of view but Virgil empathizes with the participants and finally, in the use of the metaphor *currus* which combines

---

[34] See Büchner, col. 256. Horace also used the simile of the chariot race with much the same language at *Sat.* I.1.114-116, composed around the same time (Wilkinson, 161).

[35] *Ann.* 27D, *Omnes avidi spectant ad carceris oras,/quam mox emittat pictis e faucibus currus.*

chariot, horse, and man,[36] the distinction between men and horses is blurred. Both have identical goals whereas in the previous simile they had been at variance, working separately and accomplishing nothing but ruin.

With this we may compare the narrative which precedes the simile in the *Aeneid*:

> Considunt transtris intentaque bracchia remis;
> intenti exspectant signum exsultantiaque haurit
> corda pavor pulsans laudumque arrecta cupido.
>   Inde ubi clara dedit sonitum tuba, finibus omnes,
> haut mora, prosiluere suis;

(Aen. 5.136-140)

Here, in the preparation for the race, are the empathetic lines from the narrative in the *Georgics*. *Geo.* 3.103-104 are identical to *Aen.* 5.144-145 (except for four words) and *Geo.* 3.106-107 are very close to *Aen.* 5.146-147. Virgil has deliberately omitted lines 105-106 from the simile and kept them in the narrative of the events preceding the race, just as they had been in the original passage.[37]

The stunning difference is that Virgil is using these lines not to describe an actual chariot race, but a *boat* race. By carefully making the association by means of allusion to Homer and the *Georgics*, the reader has already connected the two kinds of race, before the simile is even begun. The remainder of the *Georgics* description is then used in the simile, just as the description of the bees in *Georgics* 4 had been re-used in *Aeneid* 1 both as narrative and simile. By combining the description of the chariot-race in *Georgics* 3 with the simile in *Georgics* 1, the *Aeneid* simile becomes not so much a climax (as other similes had been), but rather a device to establish the tone for the rest of the race, which is, after all, the premier episode of the games.

In short, Virgil adds to the Homeric material the vanity of the race (*frustra*) in *Geo.* 1.513 and the hope and fear of the drivers in *Geo.* 3.105-106 and creates a simile that performs the unique function of recalling the tone and emotion of a famous Homeric contest in order to describe a quite un-Homeric one.

These 15 similes yield 19 in the *Aeneid* and all have echoes in

---

[36] For *currus* as a metaphor for horses, see Huxley, 133.

[37] In addition, at the end of the race, Virgil stresses the gaiety of the spectators rather than the results of the race.

Homer or Lucretius: Two are from Homer alone; [38] one combines two different Homeric passages; [39] two are from Homer and Lucretius; [40] and five combine Homer and Apollonius.[41] Two of the similes reverse Homer's comparand.[42] All involve a comparison with natural phenomena except *Geo.* 1.511-514 (chariot race) and 4.313 (Parthian arrows).

These similes come mainly from *Georgics* 3 and 4.[43] Eleven are in *Aeneid* 7 and 10-12, with five concentrated in Book 5. This is the opposite of the pattern found in the repeated lines, which were likewise epic, but recurred largely in Books 1, 2, 4, and 6.[44] Clearly one must conclude that these Homeric nature-similes belong to the so-called "Iliadic" books of the *Aeneid* (7-12) and to the "Iliadic" Book 5.

The major point I wish to make about these repeated similes regards their placement in the poems. Five of these similes occupy significant positions within their passages (either at the beginning, middle, or end) in the *Georgics*.[45] With the *Aeneid*, the case is different, as these repeated similes tend to reflect a more conventional Homeric comparison than their *Georgic* forebears. The chariot-race (*Geo.* 1.511-514) and the overpowering wave (3.235-241) are simply described in the *Aeneid* without any special emphasis, despite their importance in the *Georgics*. The similes of the numberless sands, the mountain, the hail and the arrows are of no particular importance in either work. In at least one occurrence in the *Aeneid*, the similes of the forest fire (*Aen.* 2.304-308) and the whirlwind have significance, but in most cases are relatively formulaic or unimportant. The similes of the birds and the smoke in the Aristaeus episode can be said to have equal importance in the *Aeneid*.

---

[38] *Geo.* 4.81, 499-500.
[39] *Geo.* 1.511-514.
[40] *Geo.* 3.237-241, 4.262.
[41] *Geo.* 2.105-106, 3.99-100, 470-471, 4.80, 261.
[42] *Geo.* 1.511-514, 4.78-81.
[43] One in Book 1, 1 in Book 2, 3 in Book 3, 5 in Book 4.
[44] Remarkably few repeated phrases recur in repeated similes, despite the similarity of subject matter. One line is nearly repeated (*Geo.* 3.237: *Aen.* 7.258) and there are only three repeated phrases of any consequence (*Geo.* 3.470: *Aen.* 2.419, *Geo.* 4.313: *Aen.* 12.856, *Geo.* 4.499: *Aen.* 5.740). This deliberate avoidance of verbal repetition would seem to argue against any of these similes being used as *tibicines*, and in favor of the careful revision Virgil gave them.
[45] *Geo.* 1.511-514, 3.99-100, 237-241, 4.313-314, 499-500.

Clearly, many of these similes, as Heinze was the first to show, have a crucial structural importance in the narrative technique of the *Aeneid*. What Heinze failed to see is that this technique is evident in the *Georgics* as well. Of course, owing to the didactic nature of the work, fewer similes are required.[46] Nevertheless, we can see in the Virgilian paragraph, as others have pointed out before me, a movement, or rising tension which either proceeds from or to an important thematic statement or *Schlussfigur*. This technique is a lineal descendant of the Lucretian digression which sought to magnify and illustrate a lesson by means of a lyrical or otherwise poetical passage.

We can say that the similes in the *Georgics* are primarily drawn from Greek epic, compare something in nature to something else in nature (as opposed to man), emphasize the human elements in natural or animal behavior and, by their infrequency and placement, have greater force in the *Georgics* than in the *Aeneid*. But the crucial fact is the difference from Homer, not merely in viewpoint (the *inscius pastor*), or comparand (the fire in the old horse, *Geo*. 3.97-100), or the addition of an empathetic detail (*sata laeta*, *Geo*. 1.325) or the combination of sources, but in the structural use of these similes to illuminate both narration and theme.

We shall see the same technique but with an important difference in the passages of narrative in the *Georgics* which are adapted for similes in the *Aeneid*.

---

[46] Particularly in the "Hesiodic" Book 1.

# CHAPTER TWO

## NARRATIVE IN THE *GEORGICS*
## USED FOR SIMILES IN THE *AENEID*

Many of the basic techniques employed in the repetition of similes from the *Georgics* in the *Aeneid* are used in the adaptation of narrative passages. I shall here concern myself with the motifs, the linkages of several similes, each reflecting on its mates as it develops an important theme.[1]

I shall take up these motifs under two headings: individuals (the tree, deer, bull, and horse) and groups (ants, birds, snakes,[2] bees and storms). Into these categories fall nearly all the similes taken from narrative in the *Georgics*.[3]

One simile that does not figure in a motif may be used to illustrate Virgil's basic use of his sources. At *Aen.* 9.59-66, Turnus, raging around the Trojan camp is compared to a wolf, lying in wait (*insidiatus*) at a full fold, roaring and enduring wind and rain while the lambs bleat under the safe protection of their mothers.

> Ac veluti pleno lupus insidiatus ovili
> quom fremit ad caulas ventos perpessus et imbris
> nocte super media: tuti sub matribus agni
> balatam exercent, ille asper et improbus ira
> saevit in absentis, collecta fatigat edendi
> ex longo rabies et siccae sanguine fauces:
> haut aliter Rutulo muros et castra tuenti
> ignescunt irae, duris dolor ossibus ardet.

---

[1] So much has been published on the motifs in the *Aeneid* as a whole and within individual books that I shall attempt no bibliography here. The important studies will be cited as necessary in the course of the chapter. I would like to note that while acknowledgement is here made to the usefulness of R. A. Hornsby's book (see Ch. I, n. 23) on motifs in the *Aeneid*, he so ignores or neglects not only the *Georgics* but also much of the influence of Homer and Apollonius that I feel my remarks here may supplement without duplicating his.

[2] Although the snake appears as an individual, this classification has been made for reasons I shall explain later.

[3] I omit the comparison to snow (*Interea toto non setius aere ninguit, Geo.* 3.367) which occurs at *Aen.* 11.610-611: *fundunt simul undique tela/crebra nivis ritu caelumque obtexitur umbra.* This is seen in *Il.* 3.222 (Odysseus' words), 12.156-157 & 278-279 (stones), and 19.357-361 (men piling off ships).

*Il.* 12.299-306 is one of the many lion similes in the *Iliad*.[4] Hector
in battle is compared to an unfed lion wanting the fattest lamb
in the fold but kept at bay all night by men and dogs. There are
no such similes of frustration involving wolves.[5] Apollonius, at
*Arg.* 1.1243ff., has Polyphemus go off like a wild animal when he
hears Hylas' cry, as if it were the bleating of a distant flock, which
the shepherds have already made safe. The sheep are in the pen
and he is left to roar in protest until he tires. But Virgil's picture
allies the rabid madness of the Homeric wolf and the maternal
fear of the ewe. Turnus is no proud lion here, but a marauding wolf
who, as he waits in patient hunger, terrifies the frightened mother
of the lambs.

This picture of the wolf may first have occurred to Virgil in
writing *Geo.* 3.537-8, part of the description of the effects of the
plague on animals and on the wolf who prowls the folds at night:

> Non lupus insidias explorat ovilia circum
> nec gregibus nocturnus obambulat:

Here *insidias* is used as *insidiatus* was in the *Aeneid*. The idea of
plotting or ambushing adds a human quality to the wolf, much as
does *obambulat*, generally used of persons. So, both Turnus and the
wolf are plotting and thus the simile not only characterizes a person
and mirrors the events of the narrative (as in Apollonius), it actually extends them both by the action it describes and by its
humanization of the wolf.

Later in the book, of course, Turnus as wolf will steal one of
the lambs, to the grief of the mother (9.565-6), linking the previous
simile, the Homeric model and the grief of Euryalus' mother
(473-497).

Virgil's humanization of animals is one of the distinguishing
features of the *Georgics*. Much of the following discussion will refer
to this humanization not simply as it occurs in the *Georgics* but as
it is transferred to and in many cases made even more powerful
and affecting in the *Aeneid*, for this is a further example of Virgilian

---

[4] Heroes on the attack are most often compared to lions (e.g. *Il.* 17.657-
664). See K. V. Hartigan, " 'He Rose Like a Lion...': Animal Similes in
Homer and Virgil", *AAntHung* 21 (1973), 224-228.
[5] Wolves work in packs in the *Iliad* similes (4.471-472, 11.72-73-Trojans
and Greeks in battle, 16.156-166-Myrmidons like wolves killing a stag,
drinking water and vomiting, 16.352-356-Greeks in battle like wolves
killing lambs).

originality. Such empathy has a forebear in Lucretius, particularly in the passage describing the distraught cow searching for her slain sacrificial calf (2.352-366). She behaves with all the anxiety of a human mother, but descriptive details never let us forget that she is an animal. When Virgil recalls this passage in his description of the plague at Noricum (*Geo.* 3.515-530), he concentrates on the grief both of the dying ox *and* of the ox's owner. He does not see the ox as if it were human (and so let the differences between the two highlight their similarities) but as a creature capable of feeling fear, grief, and a whole range of emotions obviously not confined to humans alone. In the *Aeneid*, he will draw on these implied similarities in similes that extend the comparisons beyond those of his poetic sources.

## A. Individuals

### 1. *Trees*

Botanical similes drawn from the *Georgics* are few in the *Aeneid*,[6] primarily because *Georgics* 2 contains three long digressions [7] that yield no similes. Only four similes in the *Aeneid* are drawn from this book and the only two tree similes are associated with the description of the oak in the vineyard.[8]

Trees in Homer and Apollonius are most often used in similes to compare the deaths of warriors to the felling of a tree. For example:

ἤριπε δ' ὡς ὅτε τις δρῦς ἤριπεν ἢ ἀχερωΐς,
ἠὲ πίτυς βλωθρή, τήν τ' οὔρεσι τέκτονες ἄνδρες
ἐξέταμον πελέκεσσι νεήκεσι νήϊον εἶναι·
(*Il.* 13.389-391 = 16.482-484) [9]

ἀλλ' ὡς τίς τ' ἐν ὄρεσσι πελωρίη ὑψόθι πεύκη,
τήντε θοοῖς πελέκεσσιν ἔθ' ἡμιπλῆγα λιπόντες
ὑλοτόμοι δρυμοῖο κατήλυθον· ἡ δ' ὑπὸ νυκτὶ
ῥιπῇσιν μὲν πρῶτα τινάσσεται, ὕστερον αὖτε

---

[6] There are only 15 such similes in the *Aeneid*, and four of these (the purple flower-9.435-436, the poppy-436-437, the violet-11.68-70) are very similar. *Georgics* 2 has no discussion of flowers. Their only extended mention is a recusatio against discussing them in the description of the Corycian old man's garden in *Georgics* 4.

[7] "The Praise of Italy" (136-176), "Spring" (315-345), and "The Joys of the Country Life" (458-542).

[8] Except *Aen.* 3.680, a slight simile comparing the Cyclopes to lofty oaks or cypresses. Cf. n. 14 below.

[9] See also *Il.* 5.559-560.

πρυμνόθεν ἐξαγεῖσα κατήριπεν· ὡς ὅγε ποσσὶν
ἀκαμάτοις τείως μὲν ἐπισταδὸν ἠωρεῖτο,
ὕστερον αὖτ' ἀμενηνὸς ἀπείρονι κάππεσε δούπῳ.

(Arg. 4.1682-1688)

Clearly Virgil had Apollonius' simile in mind in describing the final collapse of Troy:

> Tum vero omne mihi visum considere in ignis
> Ilium et ex imo verti Neptunia Troia:
> ac veluti summis antiquam in montibus ornum
> cum ferro accisam crebrisque bipennibus instant
> eruere agricolae certatim, illa usque minatur
> et tremefacta comam concusso vertice nutat,
> volneribus donec paulatim evicta supremum
> congemuit traxitque iugis avolsa ruinam.

(Aen. 2.624-631)

These Greek similes, which had been applied to valiant dying men, are now applied to the entire city. In other words, Troy falls like a good soldier: it threatens (*minatur*), trembles (*tremefacta*), shakes its locks (*comam nutat*), but finally, overcome by wounds (*volneribus*), it groans (*congemuit*) and falls down. Like the ash, the ancient (*antiquam*) Troy, hacked by a *bipennis* (2.479), is cut from its roots (*accisam*), an image prepared for in the description of Priam's corpse in 557, *iacet ingens litore truncus*.[10] Virgil develops from his sources in a unique way, beyond simply extending the humanization: He makes the suffering of the tree reflect that of each of Troy's fighting and dying sons. I shall have more to say on the meaning of this simile later.

For the humanizing details, Virgil may have drawn on a more immediate model, the simile in Catullus 64.105-111, describing Theseus' dispatch of the Minotaur:

> nam velut in summo quatientem brachia Tauro
> quercum aut conigeram sudanti cortice pinum
> indomitus turbo contorquens flamine robur,
> eruit (illa procul radicitus exturbata
> prona cadit, late quaevis cumque obvia frangens),[11]
> sic domito saevum prostravit corpore Theseus
> nequiquam vanis iactantem cornua ventis.

---

[10] K. J. Reckford, in "Some Trees in Virgil and Tolkien", *Perspectives of Roman Poetry: A Classics Symposium*, Austin, Texas, 1974, 65-67, has instructive comments on uprooted trees and people in the *Aeneid*.
[11] This is Robinson Ellis' reading of a very corrupt line.

Catullus is ambivalent about the species of the tree, but he stresses by geographical particularization (an Alexandrian characteristic),[12] the location of the tree, far off on the Asian massif of Taurus. The tree is humanized to an extent, but only so far as the technical terms of arboriculture may be applied to people: the tree has *bracchia* and sweats under the attack (*sudanti cortice*).[13] Thus the effect of the simile is to make the Minotaur not more human, but rather more *in*human, more a gigantic hulk than a feeling creature.

Virgil clearly remembered this description,[14] using a form of *eruere* in the identical position (preceding the trithemimeral caesura), as Catullus does, in *Geo.* 2.210, *Aen.* 2.612, 628, and 4.443. But the differences are more striking than these parallels, because Catullus' use of the simile was quite the opposite, more like Homer's than Virgil's.

But if these humanizing details are more closely observed in Virgil than in his predecessors, especially Homer, what of the original Greek similes is retained? Kenneth Reckford has aptly stated that "Homer's similes tend to help us accept the death of men in battle as natural ordinary events." [15] The cutting of the trees is not simply destructive, it has a purpose: to build ships from the lumber. In the same way in the *Aeneid*, Troy must be cut down to found Rome, the destruction is a necessary prelude to construction. As such, it recalls the clearing of the forest in *Geo.* 2.207-211: [16]

> aut unde iratus silvam devexit arator
> et nemora evertit multos ignava per annos
> antiquasque domos avium cum stirpibus imis
> eruit: illae altum nidis petiere relictis,
> at rudis enituit inpulso vomere campus.

---

[12] See M. Glass (Ch. 1, n. 24), 1-3.

[13] *Bracchia* is a proper technical term for "branches", starting with Cato (*OLD*, "bracchium", 4). *Sudo* is not used of trees before this, but the use of the specific word *cortex* dilutes the humanization. Virgil, incidentally, had used the metaphor earlier, at *Ecl.* 4.30, *quercus sudabunt* and 8.54, see below.

[14] Elsewhere, the Cyclopes stand on the shore like *aëriae quercus aut coniferae cyparissi* at *Aen.* 3.680, *corticibus sudent* occurs in *Ecl.* 8.54, Eridanus sweeps away forests *insano contorquens vertice silvas* in *Geo.* 1.481. *Coniger* is echoed by *conifer* at *Aen.* 3.680.

[15] Reckford, 64, n. 4.

[16] Trees are not cut elsewhere in the *Georgics*, but the picture of the cut trunk is used to describe Priam (*Aen.* 2.257) and Evander (11.172-175). The tree-trunk is also associated with mutilation when hung with spoils (3.286-288, 11.5-9, and most obviously, 12.766-787). See Reckford, 78. This idea of destruction preceding construction recalls Lucr. 1.262-264.

The homes of the birds are *antiquae*, like the oak, and both fall with the word *eruere*.[17] But the trees *must* be cleared and the nests destroyed to create new fields for cultivation. "Thus," as Reckford says, "Virgil's simile, applied to the city, is more painful [than similar Homeric similes], makes the event (as it was for Aeneas) more difficult to accept."[18] The difficulty lies in the fact that Virgil makes us sense the pain immediately, as do his characters, while we must learn only later that the ultimate result is positive. All the tragedies Aeneas must endure, the loss of his home, his wife, his father, and Dido, all are ultimately necessary for the final goal, the founding of Rome.

If this implicit ambivalence is drawn from Homer through the *Georgics*, there is explicit association with the *Georgics* in the other significant tree simile.

The most memorable tree simile in the *Aeneid* shows not the felling of a tree but its stubborn resistance to assault. It has a direct parallel from the *Georgics*:

> Forsitan et, scrobibus quae sint fastigia, quaeras.
> Ausim vel tenui vitem committere sulco;
> altior ac penitus terrae defigitur arbos,
> aesculus in primis, quae, quantum vertice ad auras
> aetherias, tantum radice in Tartara tendit.
> Ergo non hiemes illam, non flabra neque imbres
> convellunt; immota manet multosque nepotes,
> multa virum volvens durando saecula vincit;
> tum fortis late ramos et bracchia pandens
> huc illuc media ipsa ingentem sustinet umbram.
>
> (*Geo.* 2.288-297)

> fata obstant placidasque viri deus obstruit auris.
> Ac velut annoso validam cum robore quercum
> Alpini Boreae nunc hinc nunc flatibus illinc
> eruere inter se certant; it stridor et altae
> consternunt terram concusso stipite frondes;
> ipsa haeret scopulis et quantum vertice ad auras
> aetherias, tantum radicem in Tartara tendit:
> haud secus adsiduis hinc atque hinc vocibus heros
> tunditur et magno persentit pectore curas;
> mens immota manet, lacrimae volvontur inanes.
>
> (*Aen.* 4.440-449)

---

[17] Virgil mentions the deep roots of the trees (*stirpibus imis*) to stress their antiquity, much as he does in the description and simile of the oak.
[18] Reckford, ibid.

The comparison of men to the height of the mountain oak, the
depth of its roots and its perseverance through wind and rain is
found in the simile applied to Polypoetes and Leonteus at *Il.*
12.131-134:

τὼ μὲν ἄρα προπάροιθε πυλάων ὑψηλάων
ἕστασαν ὡς ὅτε τε δρύες οὔρεσιν ὑψικάρηνοι,
αἵ τ᾽ ἄνεμον μίμνουσι καὶ ὑετὸν ἤματα πάντα,
ῥίζῃσιν μεγάλῃσι διηνεκέεσσ᾽ ἀραρυῖαι·

As the passage on vine-planting (*Geo.* 2.273-287) concluded with
an elaborate comparison of the planting-grid with the serried ranks
of soldiers in Homeric battle [19] (279-287), so the essential didactic
point of the following passage is made in 290-291 (plant the vines
in shallow trenches but have a stout oak for support) and elaborated
in alliterative [20] reminiscence of Homer and Catullus. This expansion
allows Virgil to contrast the fragility of the vines and the shallow-
ness of the furrow with the strength and deep roots of the tree.
The great oak cools, supports, and in effect protects the vineyard
which is otherwise inhabited only by the small olive trees and
tender vines.

But the tree is more than just a protector; it is a very human
type of protector, and this humanization is prepared-for earlier in
Book 2.

The first part of the book (9-82) deals with the multiplicity of
trees found in Italy and their propagation. Virgil draws heavily
from the beginning of Book 2 of Theophrastus' *Historia Plantarum*
with some differences in arrangement [21] and some poetic touches.
The young trees have *matres* who shade them (19, 55) and from
whom they must be taken if they are to grow and produce (23).
The section on grafting continues this metaphor, as the over-
protection of the mother makes the young tree fallow (55-56);
trees have later generations (*seris nepotibus*-58); and the engrafted
tree wonders (*miratur*-82) at the strange fruit it has produced. Indeed, the grafting process is portrayed as a kind of education, [22]

---

[19] Compare 281-282 with *Il.* 19.362.

[20] Three lines begin with "A" sounds (290-292), 290 and 291 end in *arbos*
and *auras*. Alliterative phrases include *quae quantum, tantum...Tartara
tendit, immota manet, multosque,* and *virum volens vincit.*

[21] Wilkinson, 242-243.

[22] Wilkinson, 243, says that Virgil develops Theophrastus' statement
"wild things become tame by feeding and other kinds of nurture". [trans.
Wilkinson] and combines it with a similar Lucretian statement (*fructusque*

with the implied comparison of the farmer to a teacher who takes the young shoot which would otherwise, in joy at its own strength (*laeta et fortia*) rise to heaven but remain fallow (47-49). He makes it put aside its wild ways (*exuerint silvestrem animum*-51) and learn actual skills (*in quascumque voles artis haud tarda sequentur*-52). This is reiterated in line 77 where the tree must be taught to grow (*docent inolescere*).

There is far more to this section than I have mentioned. Primarily it serves to lead into the "Praise of Italy" section (136-176). But we can see Virgil establish here the figure of the shade tree as mother and the sapling as educable youth so that following the section on Italy and the variety of soils (177-258), we are prepared for the description of the oak tree.

The vineyard oak recalls the prior descriptions. It is humanized, with a *vertex* and *bracchia* and has produced *nepotes*. It rises to the heavens like the wild fallow tree and like the maternal trees, covers its charges with its shade and outlives them. But this oak is quite different. Its head may reach to heaven, but its roots strike equally deep in the underworld. Unlike the previous trees, whose purpose was production, this tree's purpose is protection.

There is also an important stylistic difference here. Rather than describe the tree in terms that specifically describe humans (*mater*, *bracchium*, *nepotes*), Virgil uses highly wrought epic language to ennoble the tree in its battle with the elements, making it stronger and longer-lived than mortals. In this way, Virgil's oak becomes as super-human as Catullus' was sub-human. By this combination of the parental, protective, and heroic, the tree acquires an aspect quite different from that of the maternal shade trees, whose coverage kills her young shoots. The shade of the oak *protects* its charges as it endures the mighty assaults of nature, and should therefore be considered masculine and, probably, paternal, the *paterfamilias* of the vineyard.[23]

---

*feros mansuescere terra/cernebant indulgendo blandeque colendo*-5.1368-1369) to make *fructusque feros mollite colendo*. Ovid echoes these words in his definition of the purposes of an education in the humanities, *emollit mores nec sinit esse feros* (*Epis. ex Pont.* 2.9.48).

[23] For the protective vine, not tree, associated with the father of the house, see Aesch. *Ag.* 966-969 (of Agamemnon), with son and heir, see Soph. *Ant.* 600, ἐσχάτας ὑπὲρ/ῥίζας ὃ τέτατο φάος ἐν Οἰδίπου δόμοις, and with mother earth, Pindar, *Pyth.* 9.9, ῥίζαν...θάλλοισαν.

The oak is used, amid a complex of intricately woven images,[24] in *Aeneid* 4 to describe *pater Aeneas* enduring the final pleas of Anna. Like Catullus' Asian tree, this Alpine oak, nestled in crags (not in a field like the vineyard oak), is shown actually enduring the buffeting storm. But while Catullus' locale had enforced the foreignness of the Minotaur both geographically and biologically, Virgil's location of the tree stresses its unprotected isolation. Expressive sound patterns are joined to expressive metrical devices to emphasize and to an extent re-create the blasts.[25]

Because of the requirements of the simile, Virgil stresses the battling winds which may represent the opposing wishes of both mortals and divinities, but the focus of the simile is clearly on the tree as a surrogate Aeneas, actually struggling against the storm. Like Aeneas, it is of an age (*annoso*), it groans (*it stridor*),[26] and seems to weep as it shakes its leaves and lets them fall (*altae/consternunt terram concusso stipite frondes*), much as Aeneas grieves (*persentit pectore curas*) and seems to weep (*lacrimae volvontur inanes*).[27] The roots descending to Tartarus may prefigure Aeneas' trip to the Underworld, the lofty branches his apotheosis. They may also show the sources of his security in enduring the onslaught: his father, wife, and ancestors now reside in the Underworld, while usually, his mother lives in Olympus.

On the one hand, we are, as has been pointed out, meant to see in this simile a direct contrast with the happy first meeting of Jason and Medea in Apollonius *Arg.* 3.967-972:[28]

---

[24] See F. L. Newton, "Recurrent Imagery in *Aeneid* 4" *TAPA* 88 (1957), 31-43. For a discussion of fire imagery, see B. Fenik, "Parallelism of Theme and Imagery in *Aeneid* II and IV" *AJP* 80 (1959), 1-24.

[25] I.e. the dactyls in 441, the hard "c" sounds and spondees of 442, line 443 is split in half while the buffeting ceases before the roar, followed by the heavy spondee and "c" and "t" sounds in 444 as the beating of the tree resumes.

[26] Servius says *it stridor* "*ad dolorem Aeneae pertinet de quo ait* (4.448) '*magno persentit pectore curas.*' " It does not refer to the general din of the storm but specifically to the sound made by the object upon which the action is directed, like the rigging of the ships in 1.87, the chains in 6.558, the bees in 7.65, and the javelin in 11.863.

[27] Anna weeps and Aeneas *may* weep (on the strength of the simile) and we surely imagine that Dido has a share of the weeping as well. The notion in this line is one of general sorrow at the conflict of love and duty. See Austin, IV, 135, R. D. Williams, *The Aeneid of Virgil Books 1-6*, London, 1972, 373. *Volvuntur* may recall *volvens* from 2.295. On the varied uses of *volvere* in Virgil, see G. Williams, 739, and Perkins (Ch. I, n. 10), 270.

[28] Otis, 73-76.

τὼ δ' ἄνεῳ καὶ ἄναυδοι ἐφέστασαν ἀλλήλοισιν,
ἢ δρυσίν, ἢ μακρῇσιν ἐειδόμενοι ἐλάτῃσιν,
αἵτε παρᾶσσον ἔκηλοι ἐν οὔρεσιν ἐρρίζωνται,
νηνεμίῃ· μετὰ δ' αὖτις ὑπὸ ῥιπῆς ἀνέμοιο
κινύμεναι ὁμάδησαν ἀπείριτον· ὡς ἄρα τώγε
μέλλον ἅλις φθέγξασθαι ὑπὸ πνοιῇσιν Ἔρωτος.

Aeneas is no flexible young sapling, swaying as the breezes take him in innocent and careless joy. He is now a mature oak who cannot afford to be swayed by the assaulting breezes as he must force the bitter break with Dido. This simile not only reverses the terms of Apollonius' oak trees, but links with Virgil's previous simile of the ash.

Line 440 is crucial: it is fate and heaven's sanction that Aeneas endure. The fateful element coupled with the detail of the winds blowing from all sides (plus the echo of *concusso vertice* in *concusso stipite*) recalls both the battling winds simile (*Aen.* 2.416-418) and the rowan hacked by the farmers already discussed, both used to describe the fall of Troy.

We now see that while the felled ash was on one level representative of the fall of Troy, on another level it represents the idea of a strong and stable home collapsed into ruin, as perceived by Aeneas himself (*mihi visum-Aen.* 2.624). This strength and stability revived is represented by Aeneas in Book 4. Having been entrusted with the *sacra* and *deos* of Troy (2.293), he now becomes their embodiment. *Pater Aeneas* is represented by the paternal oak tree, protective and enduring, and this element, essential to the tree motif in the *Aeneid*, comes directly from the earlier description in the *Georgics*.

The association of the tree with Troy is continued in Book 7.59-67 in the portent of the bees swarming into a laurel tree in Latinus' *penetralia*. The tree is *sacra comam multosque metu servata per annos* (60) and by supplying a home for the bees, it presages the founding of the new Troy in Latium.[29]

The Italian people are described in *Aen.* 8.313-315 as sprung from trees themselves (*gensque virum truncis et duro robore nata*-315) and are led by a succession of exiles, first Saturn, then Evander, then Aeneas and finally Augustus.[30] Line 315 is a direct echo of

---

[29] Reckford, 72.

[30] On the structure of this *aition*, see E. V. George, *Aeneid VIII and the Aitia of Callimachus* (*Mnemosyne* Supplement, 27), Leiden, 1974, 82-84.

*Geo.* 1.63, *unde homines nati, durum genus,* describing the men created from the stones thrown by Deucalion, in turn echoing Hesiod, *Works* 143-145, in which Zeus creates the bronze race of men ἐκ μελιᾶν.

This race originally sprung from wood will at last be governed by wood, the sceptre of Latinus, which is described in much the same terms as the ash and the oak: [31]

> 'numquam fronde levi fundet virgulta nec umbras,
> cum semel in silvis imo de stirpe recisum
> matre caret posuitque comas et bracchia ferro,
> olim arbos, nunc artificis manus aere decoro
> inclussit patribusque dedit gestare Latinis.'
>
> (*Aen.* 12.207-211)

Here the tree, like Troy, is uprooted, has lost its family, and has lost its *bracchia* and *comae*. The degree of sympathy is almost overworked. But as with the ash, the young tree was sacrificed to a noble cause. The governance of Latium, which the sceptre represents, is worth the loss of a tree, as the establishment of Rome is worth the loss of Troy. The tree now comes to stand for all that Aeneas has struggled for. Virgil thus transforms what had been a purely poetic image of paternal strength and security into a literal symbol carried by the "fathers of Latium" (*patribus...Latinis*). For it must be remembered that the description of the sceptre occurs in a simile, Latinus vowing that his word is unshakeable and no more able to be swayed than the sceptre is able to bear leaves. The language he uses to describe his resolve recalls the oak simile and Aeneas' storm at sea:

> nec me vis ulla volentem
> avertet, non, si tellurem effundat in undas
> diluvio miscens caelumque in Tartara solvat,
>
> (*Aen.* 12.203-205)

Tree and man are now united by their common sacrifice, stability, and sturdiness, as the future harmony of Latins and Trojans becomes assured.

We can see then that the patience and fatherly protectiveness of the tree in the *Georgics* developed from Homer's simple description of height and sacrifice along with Apollonius' and Catullus'

---

[31] The scene is drawn from Achilles' oath in *Il.* 1.233-244. See Reckford, 79-80.

humanizing details and forms the basis for a motif in the *Aeneid*
which links the permanence and patience of the tree to the destiny
of Rome.[32]

### 2. *Large Animals: Deer*

intereunt pecudes, stant circumfusa pruinis
corpora magna boum confertoque agmine cervi
torpent mole nova et summis vix cornibus extant.
Hos non immissis canibus, non cassibus ullis
puniceaeve agitant pavidos formidine pennae,
sed frustra oppositum trudentis pectore montem
comminus obtruncant ferro graviterque rudentis
caedunt et magno laeti clamore reportant.

*(Geo.* 3.368-375)


saepe volutabris pulsos silvestribus apros
latratu turbabis agens, montisque per altos
ingentem clamore premes ad retia cervom.

*(Geo.* 3.411-413)


Uritur infelix Dido totaque vagatur
urbe furens, qualis coniecta cerva sagitta,
quam procul incautam nemora inter Cresia fixit
pastor agens telis liquitque volatile ferrum
nescius: illa fuga silvas saltusque peragrat
Dictaeos; haeret lateri letalis harundo.

*(Aen.* 4.68-73)


inclusum veluti si quando flumine nanctus
cervom aut puniceae saeptum formidine pinnae
venator cursu canis et latratibus instat;
ille autem insidiis et ripa territus alta
mille fugit refugitque vias, at vividus Umber
haeret hians, iam iamque tenet similisque tenenti
increpuit malis morsuque elusus inani est;
tum vero exoritur clamor ripaeque lacusque
responsant circa et caelum tonat omne tumultu.

*(Aen.* 12.749-757)

---

[32] I pass over the objections to the similes in the *Georgics* (by Page) and
the *Aeneid* (by Sparrow) that they are unprepared-for or out-of-place.
While there is some truth to this in the *Aeneid*, the question does not alter
my basic contentions.

A group of Trojans surround Odysseus in *Il.* 11.473-484: [33]

εὗρον ἔπειτ' Ὀδυσῆα διίφιλον ἀμφὶ δ' ἄρ' αὐτὸν
Τρῶες ἕπονθ' ὡς εἴ τε δαφοινοὶ θῶες ὄρεσφιν
ἀμφ' ἔλαφον κεραὸν βεβλημένον, ὅν τ' ἔβαλ' ἀνὴρ
ἰῷ ἀπὸ νευρῆς· τὸν μέν τ' ἤλυξε πόδεσσι
φεύγων, ὄφρ' αἷμα λιαρὸν καὶ γούνατ' ὀρώρῃ·
αὐτὰρ ἐπεὶ δὴ τόν γε δαμάσσεται ὠκὺς ὀϊστός,
ὠμοφάγοι μιν θῶες ἐν οὔρεσι δαρδάπτουσιν
ἐν νέμεϊ σκιερῷ· ἐπί τε λῖν ἤγαγε δαίμων
σίντην· θῶες μέν τε διέτρεσαν, αὐτὰρ ὁ δάπτει·
ὣς ῥα τότ' ἀμφ' Ὀδυσῆα δαΐφρονα ποικιλομήτην
Τρῶες ἕπον πολλοί τε καὶ ἄλκιμοι, αὐτὰρ ὅ γ' ἥρως
ἀΐσσων ᾧ ἔγχει ἀμύνετο νηλεὲς ἦμαρ.

Apollonius also describes an event in a deer hunt at *Arg.* 2.278-283, comparing it to the attack on the Harpies by Zetes and Calais:

ὡς δ' ὅτ' ἐνὶ κνημοῖσι κύνες δεδαημένοι ἄγρης
ἢ αἶγας κεραοὺς ἠὲ πρόκας ἰχνεύοντες
θείωσιν, τυτθὸν δὲ τιταινόμενοι μετόπισθεν
ἄκρης ἐν γενύεσσι μάτην ἀράβησαν ὀδόντας·
ὣς Ζήτης Κάλαΐς τε μάλα σχεδὸν ἀΐσσοντες
τάων ἀκροτάτῃσιν ἐπέχραον ἤλιθα χερσίν.

Virgil clearly recalls the Homeric hunt-similes in *Geo.* 3.369-375, but with significant changes: humans, not jackals or hounds are doing the hunting and the hunt is no challenge to the hunters at all. The stranded deer are buried up to their horns in the snow and are numbed out of action by the unusual morass (*torpent mole nova*). Their vain struggle (*frustra*) and sad death-moans (*graviter rudentis*) are contrasted with the happy whoops of the hunters (*magno laeti clamore*) who, having slain the deer, begin a joyous winter celebration (376-380). The principal addition to Homer is the ambivalent Virgilian sympathy: the pathetic deer must be killed to feed the men. Our sadness for the victims should balance our joy for the hunters; both are victims of the cruel German winter.

---

[33] Compare *Il.* 22.189-192, a shortened version of the simile quoted here. Deer occur in Homeric similes as passive groups to which the fearfulness of the Trojan troops (*Il.* 11.113-121, 13.101-104, 21.29, 22.1), the Greek troops (in a taunt by Agamemnon-4.240-249), or the suitors (*Od.* 4.335-340, 17.126-131) is compared. See Hartigan, 230-231. The only other deer simile compares the body of Kebriones to that of a slain deer over which lions fight, *Il.* 16.756-761.

The two obstacles to Aeneas' successful fulfillment of his fate are compared to deer: Dido in *Aeneid* 4 and Turnus in 12.

The simile of the wounded doe has been thoroughly discussed in conjunction with the intricate pattern of similes in the book by others [34] and I shall not recount their findings here. The simile itself derives from the Homeric similes quoted above, the application of such a simile to lovers derives from Apollonius, *Arg.* 4.11-13:

Τῇ δ' ἀλεγεινότατον κραδίῃ φόβον ἔμβαλεν ¨Ηρη·
τρέσσεν δ', ἠύτε τις κούφη κεμάς, ἥντε βαθείης
τάρφεσιν ἐν ξυλόχοιο κυνῶν ἐφόβησεν ὁμοκλή.

Here, as Otis says, the simile conveys, by its combination of Apollonian and Homeric elements, the notion of tragic, doomed love.[35] Despite the principal application of the simile to Dido, Virgil adds an ambivalence, a sympathy for both the *pastor* who is *nescius* and the deer who is *incauta* of the arrow and its consequences. This double sympathy for hunter and prey who are both victimized by forces beyond their control (either misfortune or the will of Venus and Juno) is very like the feeling for both the Germans and the deer in the *Georgics*, whose actions are the result of the exigencies of weather.

Beyond this similar subjectivity, there are few parallels either verbal or otherwise between the passages in the *Georgics* and the simile in the *Aeneid*.

The second of the quoted *Aeneid* similes, like its Homeric model, describes the combat of the major heroes, Aeneas and Turnus. The simile is significant in two ways: Aeneas is here compared for only the fourth time in the poem to an animal,[36] his frustration reducing his heroic stature, and Turnus, who had been described as an aggressive animal,[37] is compared to a frightened and cornered quarry.

The simile may be divided into four parts: 752-753, from Homer (the deer is terrified of the traps and bank but also of the dogs

---

[34] Newton, 31-43, Otis, 71-88, and J. Ferguson, "Fire and Wound: the Imagery of *Aeneid* iv. 1ff.", *PVS* 10 (1970-1971), 57-63.

[35] Otis, 78.

[36] Twice in Book 2, at 355 (wolf) and 374 (snake) during the frenzy of Troy's fall, and twice in Book 12, at 715-724 (bull) and this passage.

[37] At 9.59 (wolf), 563 (eagle), 563 (wolf), 729 (tiger), 791 (lion), 10.454 (lion), 11.491 (horse), 12.4 (lion), 101 (bull), 133 (horse), 715 (bull). (Hartigan, 243).

and flees far—*mille fugit refugitque vias*—not simply "through glens and glades"); 753-755, the dog gnashing his teeth in vain, from Apollonius; the flanking sections, 749-751 and 756-757 from the *Georgics*, the stag (not fawn or deer) trapped *formidine pennae*. There is no hunter in the simile, a single dog opposes the deer (as the boar in *Geo.* 4.11ff.) and the final din (*exoritur clamor*) is not the joy of the hunters, but the frustration of the yapping dog.

While Homer's simile had involved two actions, the running of the stag, then the capture of its corpse by a lion, Virgil, as in the *Georgics*, stresses not action, but two emotions in this simile, the fear of the stag at his entrapment and pointless struggle, then the frustration of the dog who almost has his quarry in his teeth. There is a further ambivalence: Turnus, while pathetic, arouses no sympathy; he must die as the deer trapped in the snow in the *Georgics* must die; Aeneas, his nobility diminished for the moment by his frustration, is, in the words of Putnam, "nothing but a savage dog, preparing to devour his hapless victim." [38] Perhaps they are reduced to this savagery by the necessity of fulfilling their fates. In any event, both characters seem somewhat victimized by consequences here.

In short, the alteration from a double comparison of action in Homer to emotion in Virgil and the reduction of the participants to a less than noble animal state are particularly Virgilian and seem to have their source in the *Georgics*. Significant verbal parallels, however, are lacking.[39]

### 3. *Cattle and Horses*

One major difference between the first and second books of the *Georgics* is the shift from inanimate to animate subjects. In Book 3, Virgil ostensibly ignores man altogether while stressing what is in many ways the essential similarity of man and the beasts.

Virgil first describes cattle in terms of positive, constructive love: The oxen are members of a family, the male leader of which is a *maritus* (175) or *pater* (138), the female is a *mater* (51ff., 138) and the young are not *vituli* or *pulli*, but *nati* (128), whose training

---

[38] M. C. J. Putnam, *The Poetry of the Aeneid*, Cambridge, Mass., 1964, 189.

[39] *Agens* (*Geo.* 3.412: *Aen.* 4.70) is used to describe the chasing; 4.72, *silvas saltusque peragrat* comes from *Geo.* 4.53 (with a change of number), describing the happy bees. But this is the extent of the reminiscences of this kind.

is outlined in terms of human education (163-165).[40] Virgil attributes to the animals the human emotions of shame, ambition, and grief while the species takes on a particular character that is patient, loyal and friendly. But both horses and cattle are susceptible to the pernicious form of love, sexual passion.

Virgil deals in the next section at some length with the selection of the most promising stallion for racing, fighting, and breeding. Boldness, spirit, and a competitive nature are the most desirable qualities. A horse that possesses these can then be taught to endure the exigencies of domesticated life and to develop a desire for the praise of human beings. The trained horse, although broken and schooled, is still dangerous when given its head and is compared to a storm wind on the loose (196-201). The attributes that, combined, make this horse a successful racer or war-horse are connected with the intensity of its sexual desire. Homer stresses sexual desire (and vanity) in his most elaborate horse-simile used here to describe Paris and again, at *Il.* 15.263-268, to describe Hector:

ὡς δ' ὅτε τις στατὸς ἵππος, ἀκοστήσας ἐπὶ φάτνῃ,
δεσμὸν ἀπορρήξας θείῃ πεδίοιο κροαίνων,
εἰωθὼς λούεσθαι ἐϋρρεῖος ποταμοῖο,
κυδιόων· ὑψοῦ δὲ κάρη ἔχει, ἀμφὶ δὲ χαῖται
ὤμοις ἀΐσσονται· ὁ δ' ἀγλαΐηφι πεποιθώς,
ῥίμφα ἑ γοῦνα φέρει μετά τ' ἤθεα καὶ νομὸν ἵππων·
ὡς υἱὸς Πριάμοιο Πάρις κατὰ Περγάμου ἄκρης
τεύχεσι παμφαίνων ὥς τ' ἠλέκτωρ ἐβεβήκει
καγχαλόων, ταχέες δὲ πόδες φέρον·

(*Il.* 6.506-514)

Here the free-spirited horse exults in his freedom, freed from the manger and making for the mares. This simile is also used by Ennius, as Macrobius (6.3.7) tells us:

Et tum sicut equus qui de praesepibus fartus
vincla suis magnis animis abrupit et inde
fert sese campi per caerula laetaque prata
celso pectore; saepe iubam quassat simul altam;
spiritus ex anima calida spumas agit albas,

(*Ann.* 514-518V)

---

[40] He also speaks of the maiden cow having a proper marriage ceremony (*aetas Lucinam iustosque pati hymenaeos*-60). For these parallels and many others for which I am indebted, see W. Liebeschuetz, "Beast and Man in the Third Book of Virgil's *Georgics*", *G & R*, 12 (1965), 64-77.

Ennius adds to Homer (and Apollonius 2.1259-1261) the description of the foam at the mouth, shifting the focus from sexuality to more general ferocity.[41]

Virgil treats the sexuality of the stallions after his main discussion of raising horses, and leaves his most fearsome description of carnal frenzy for the mare (*scilicet ante omnis furor est insignis equarum*-266). But he does portray the horse released from his training:

> tum cursibus auras,
> tum vocet ac per aperta volans ceu liber habenis
> aequora vix summa vestigia ponat harena,
>
> (*Geo.* 3.193-195)

Here the emphasis is on the horse's exultant speed, much as in the earlier description of the chariot-race (*Geo.* 3.103-112) and the other Homeric horse-similes.[42]

Virgil goes on to describe the irrational and often self-destructive behavior caused by the sexual impulse (209-283). From his didactic sources [43] he selects the animal descriptions which demonstrate most clearly the terrible effects of *amor*. Not only are the animals humanized, but to examples of bulls and horses destroyed by passion is added an example of a human so affected, Leander (258-263). Worst of all is the madness of the mares who, crazed by *hippomanes*, are capable even of killing their master when they are denied satisfaction of their lust. (267-268) Man must control the sexual passion of animals and turn it to useful ends by allowing male animals access to females only at times advantageous for breeding.

In this section, Virgil gives a vignette of the bulls who, previously so domestic, are now afflicted by passion. The bull wastes away at the sight of the cow who charms him *dulcibus...inlecebris*, and is driven by her into a duel with a rival (212-218). This humanization is heavily mock-heroic, a change in tone from the previous didactic descriptions. The ensuing battle of the bulls (220-223), the exile of

---

[41] G. Williams (695) sees the shift removing "all sense of the effeminate".

[42] *Il.* 22.21-24 (Achilles runs like a chariot horse), 162-166 (Achilles and Hector circle Troy like chariots rounding a turn in a race), *Od.* 13.81-85 (Odysseus' boat is as fast as a team of horses).

[43] The battle of the bulls in *Geo.* 3.219-241 and the following passage draw on Aristotle's *Historia Animalium*, but there is also material from Varro. See P. Jahn, "Aus Vergils Dichterwerkstätte, *Georgica* III, 49-470", *RhM* 60 (1905), 361-387.

the unrequited loser (224-234), and his training and subsequent victory (235-241) carry the tone yet further.

These descriptions of the horse and bull affected by *amor* are used in the *Aeneid* in books 11 and 12 to describe Turnus. Of these, the horse may be of special interest, both because it was a symbol of Carthage, Aeneas' other obstacle to success,[44] and because of the spirited white steeds which portended war and peace for the Trojans in the omen interpreted by Anchises.[45] Turnus becomes the single embodiment of these war horses toward the end of the Latin War when, dressed for battle and exulting in his courage, he is described: [46]

> qualis ubi abruptis fugit praesepia vinclis
> tandem liber ecus campoque potitus aperto
> aut ille in pastus armentaque tendit equarum
> aut adsuetus aquae perfundi flumine noto
> emicat arrectisque fremit cervicibus alte
> luxurians luduntque iubae per colla, per armos.
>
> (*Aen.* 11.492-497)

The comparison of the boldness of the soldiers and the sexuality of the stallion all go back to Homer.[47] But there is an added resonance, for, as the simile had been applied to Paris and Hector in the *Iliad*, it necessarily implies the doom of the vainglorious and reckless Turnus.[48]

The horse in the *Georgics* has been trained by its master (187-193) and Virgil stresses that it can only be released after this training (*tum...tum*-193-194). When this time comes, it is made to run free ("challenge the winds") but only *as if* free from its reins (*ceu liber habenis*); it is still under its master's control.

Turnus, however, is compared to a horse who has likewise been

---

[44] At *Aen.* 1.444. On this, see E. Kraggerud, "Vergil über die Gründung Karthagos", *SO* 38 (1963), 32-37.

[45] *Aen.* 3.536-543. Turnus has white steeds at 12.84.

[46] This is really the only horse simile in the *Aeneid*: two others involve comparison with chariots, as in Homer (n. 42 above), 5.146 and 12.333. The horse motif as applied to Turnus, however, continues.

[47] Apollonius, *Arg.* 3.1259-1262, omits the sexual reference in describing Jason in battle:

ὡς δ' ὅτ' ἀρήιος ἵππος ἐελδόμενος πολέμοιο
σκαρθμῷ ἐπιχρεμέθων κρούει πέδον, αὐτὰρ ὕπερθεν
κυδιόων ὀρθοῖσιν ἐπ' οὔασιν αὐχέν' ἀείρει·
τοῖος ἄρ' Αἰσονίδης ἐπαγαίετο κάρτεϊ γυίων.

[48] W. S. Anderson, "Vergil's Second *Iliad*", *TAPA*, 88 (1957), 28.

restrained for some time (*tandem*), but who has burst not reins but chains (*abruptis... vinclis*). The obvious parallel of this simile is the Homeric simile quoted above. But in that passage, the horse had simply been feeding, left its manger (506) and broken its halter (507). Virgil's horse is not only free, it is out of control. The verbal reminiscence in 493 (*liber... campoque aperto*) must be intended to recall *aperto... liber aequora* and point up the contrast of the two situations: in the *Georgics*, the horse is flying over the open plain, but not really free; in the *Aeneid*, the horse is free, but does not run off wildly. Ironically, Turnus' girding of himself has been a release of his pent-up frustration. Virgil eliminates the causes of the restraint (feeding in Homer, training in the *Georgics*) and instead concentrates on the sheer exultation Turnus feels in his new courage and hope (*animis et spe*). He adds the political notion (*potitus aperto*), as if to say that Turnus is temporarily master of the land he is fighting for. He then combines the element of sexuality in 494 (stated in the *Iliad*, implied in the *Georgics*) with the pure joyful release of running from the *Georgics*.

The comparison with the horse has three points: 1) with the treaty broken, there is no longer any constraint against Turnus fighting for Lavinia; 2) he is beautiful in his armor; 3) in his strength and arrogance, he is as fearsome as a horse in the throes of *amor*.[49] But, in the light of the description of the horse in the *Georgics*, the sinister implications of bursting his chains reveal the man ruled by love and rage for glory, irrational and destructive forces in a dangerous situation, reminiscent of the chariots out of control at the end of *Georgics* 1. Turnus embodies here the darker side of the stallion's high spirit, not mentioned in the *Georgics*.

At *Aen.* 12.64-70, Turnus, having rejected the rational arguments of Latinus (43-44, 54-63), is inflamed by the sight of Lavinia (*illum turbat amor, figitque in virgine vultus*-70) and, at the height of his passion, is inflamed by the sight of his chargers:

> poscit equos gaudetque tuens ante ora frementis,
> Pilumno quos ipsa decus dedit Orithyia,
> qui candore nives anteirent, cursibus auras;

> (*Aen.* 12.82-84)

[49] Love in the Homeric similes had simply been representative of a wild, irrational passion; that specific emotion had no correspondent in the simile of Paris pursuing Hector or the simile of Hector urging his charioteers to battle. *Amor* is present in this and the following associations of Turnus as the horse or bull.

His horses are white, like those that had portended war in *Aeneid* 3 and they are swift in comparison with the wind, like those in *Geo.* 3.196-201. Turnus' strength and sexuality are here stressed by the simile with the addition of his affection and admiration for these creatures he so resembles.

Finally, at *Aen.* 12.365-369, Turnus is compared to the very kind of storm-wind to which the speed of the horses had been compared in *Geo.* 3.196-201.

A third comparison of Turnus to an animal leaves little doubt that the description in this passage as a whole (12.1-133, the formation of the treaty) intentionally echoes material in the *Georgics*. In *Aen.* 12.103-106, as Turnus works himself into a rage against Aeneas, he is compared to a bull that prepares himself for battle. The depiction of the combat between the two heroes is drawn directly from the description of the battle of the bulls in *Geo.* 3.219-223.

In the two battles, the bulls fight for a heifer (*Geo.* 3.215ff.) while the heroes fight for, among other things, the hand of Lavinia (cf. 9.137). They deal many wounds:

> illi alternantes multa vi proelia miscent (*Geo.* 3.220)
> illi inter sese multa vi vulnera miscent (*Aen.* 12.720)

They bathe themselves in blood:

> lavit ater corpora sanguis (*Geo.* 3.221)
> sanguine largo/colla armosque lavant (*Aen.* 12.721-722)

They butt each other:

> versaque in obnixos urguentur cornua vasto (*Geo.* 3.222)
> cornuaque obnixi infigunt (*Aen.* 12.721)

and the woods and hills re-echo their groans:

> reboant silvaeque et longus Olympus (*Geo.* 3.223)
> gemitu nemus omne remugit (*Aen.* 12.722)

The changes made between these two similes are largely determined by subject-matter.[50] The action is very similar, and it must

---

[50] In *Aen.* 12.720, *inter sese* is virtually synonymous with *alternantes*, but it stresses the thrusts back and forth between them. *Proelia* reinforces the idea that the bulls are having a *battle*, and it helps to humanize them. Turnus and Aeneas exchange *vulnera*, a more vivid word. The two men as bulls wash both their necks and their arms in blood, where the bulls wash their bodies in blood. All of Olympus resounds in the *Georgics*, but only the whole grove in the *Aeneid*.

be remembered that, while the contest in the *Aeneid* is between essentially political enemies, Turnus and Aeneas are also social and emotional enemies as were the bulls in the *Georgics*.

The bull in the *Georgics* goes into exile after his disgraceful defeat and learns to put his anger into his horns by charging at tree trunks.[51] He returns to fight his unmindful rival and, we assume, overpower him. In the *Aeneid*, 12.104-106, Turnus does the same, but in a reversed order [52] (in lines repeated exactly from *Geo.* 3.232-234).[53] In the *Georgics*, the simile gives the result of its action (the overpowering wave symbolizes the bull's victory), while in the *Aeneid*, the denouement of the action is carried out in the narrative.[54]

The placement and effect of these similes has been set forth by Klingner.[55] These similes follow passages of narrative which build up the rage of Turnus or the power of the combat between the two heroes to the point where a simile is introduced to isolate and magnify the subjective feeling of the participants or onlookers. Similarly, the passage on the bull in *Georgics* 3 ends with a simile comparing the charging bull to an overpowering wave that sweeps all before it.[56]

We turn finally to Dido. The first two lines of *Aeneid* 4 describe her growing love in terms used of the passion of love (and also of the plague) in *Georgics* 3. She has fire in her veins both here and at 23, 54, and 66, and madness in her bones at 101, as did the mare (*flamma medullis-Geo.* 3.271). There is no rest for her limbs and she wanders about the city (*vagatur urbe-Aen.* 4.68-69) as the hippomanes-crazed mare had wandered over pastures and fields in her passion and the lioness had strayed from her fold (*erravit-Geo.*

---

[51] Compare the boar in *Geo.* 3.255-257.

[52] Putnam, 185, notices this. He also finds that the simile concerns "not only the battle itself but its effect on the world at large" 184). The verbal parallel of *Turnus-taurus* is set in 7.783, *Ipse inter primas praestanti corpore Turnus*, an echo of *Geo.* 4.538, *quattuor eximios praestanti corpore tauros*.

[53] Also drawn from *Geo.* 3.233-234 is *Aen.* 5.377, the bull striking the air with his horns as does Dares with his fists: *ventos lacessit/ictibus; verberat ictibus auras*. But this is not a simile.

[54] Compare the descriptions of the oak tree above. Putnam says of the battle in the *Georgics*, "We do not learn the outcome". (p. 185)

[55] F. Klingner, *Virgil: Bucolica Georgica Aeneis*, Zurich & Stuttgart, 1967, 289.

[56] Black sand here parallels the yellow sand kicked up by the contending horses in the chariot race, *Geo.* 3.110.

3.246). This wandering is picked up in the simile of the wounded doe (*Aen.* 4.69-73) who, struck by the arrow of a hunter, runs through fields and groves. This simile also reminds us of the peaceful stags in the *Georgics* who go to unwonted war when love strikes them (265).

At *Aen.* 4.86-89, all the work of building Carthage ceases, as Virgil had said that cattle and horses and lionness became unmindful of their proper responsibilities when in love. *Aen.* 4.133-135 show Dido's proud horse stomping about and arching his neck. At 265-276 the forgetful lover Aeneas is scolded by Mercury because his dalliance at Carthage has caused him to neglect his mission to found Rome. Mercury calls him *oblitus* (267), the word Virgil had used for the lionness (*Geo.* 3.245).

At the height of her tragedy, Dido stands raging upon a tower, unmarried, but calling on her "husband" Aeneas. The horse, in the *Georgics*, without wedlock, stood on a crest to sniff the breezes. In her final taunt to Aeneas, Dido calls herself *moritura* in a line directly taken from the Hero and Leander tale, *nec moritura semper crudeli funere Dido* (308). And finally, she draws from among the potions and spells of her witchcraft, in her final desperate hours, the dread *hippomanes* (515-516).

The meaning and effects of these references to the *Georgics* should be clear. But this does not mean by any stretch that Virgil drew his characterization of Dido from his depiction of the mare, any more than he drew Turnus and Aeneas from the bulls. Instead, he used elements from the prior poem to point up a theme common to the two: passion is dangerous and particularly so with high-spirited females. What I wish to show is that the impulses that drive these men and animals, the extremes of behavior to which they go, and the often tragic end to which they succumb, are similar in both poems and show a unified conception of sexual passion which develops in the later poem but shares many traits with that of the animals in the *Georgics*.

I would not say that Virgil could not have written this or even more derivative parts of the *Aeneid* without the *Georgics*. Too often, those who note comparative passages between the two have shown how the *Aeneid* is indebted to the *Georgics*. Instead, I would stress not the derivativeness of the *Aeneid* but the originality of the *Georgics*. Virgil added, in selecting material from the handbooks of Varro and others, the amatory impulse which is evident in the similes of Homer and Apollonius and in the mythological

examples which he supplies. It is not at all odd that such similes
and allusions should occur in the *Aeneid*. But that they should
occur in the *Georgics at all* is unique and has gone largely unnoticed.

To sum up, Virgil's implicit comparison of animals to humans in
the *Georgics* is mirrored in the similes of the *Aeneid* that compare
men to animals. Such comparisons show that he was painfully
aware of the bestiality that lurks close under the surface control
of civilized humans. He intends more than a simple rapprochement
of the personalities of men and the nobler animals. Control of the
bestial impulses is the crucial factor which determines whether
these powerful forces will be turned to good purpose or fulfill
their destructive potential.

It was perhaps the turbulence of Virgil's times which gave rise
to his fears and repeated warnings (throughout the *Georgics*) about
the ever-present danger inherent in the animal side of man. In the
*Georgics*, Virgil is concerned with the entire lifespan of the animals,
their birth, growth, and death, and he cannot fully develop the human
theme. In the *Aeneid*, however, the subject is civilized man and
by portraying men who are susceptible to passion for political or
emotional ends, Virgil shows men suffering the consequences of
their animal natures.

## B. Groups

### 1. *Ants*

Similes involving small animals (ants, birds, snakes, and bees)
employ the same techniques as the similes of the larger animals,
especially humanization and structural integration into the poem.
Larger animals tend to stand for an abstract characteristic of an
individual (fear, love, jealousy), while the smaller animals are
portrayed always in groups and so represent societal characteristics.
As such, the descriptions of smaller animals resemble their Homeric
counterparts more than do the latter. To point out these differences,
let us examine the description of the ants.

Virgil portrays the animals that can inhabit the threshing floor:

> saepe exiguus mus
> sub terris posuitque domos atque horrea fecit,
> aut oculis capti fodere cubilia talpae,
> inventusque cavis bufo et quae plurima terrae
> monstra ferunt, populatque ingentem farris acervom
> curculio atque inopi metuens formica senectae.
>
> (*Geo.* 1.181-186)

At *Aen.* 4.393ff., the Trojans prepare to set sail from Carthage. They ready the ships and stream from all over the city bringing supplies. Virgil then compares them to ants:

> Migrantis cernas totaque ex urbe ruentis:
> ac velut ingentem formicae farris acervom
> cum populant hiemis memores tectoque reponunt,
> it nigrum campis agmen praedamque per herbas
> convectant calle angusto; pars grandia trudunt
> obnixae frumenta umeris, pars agmina cogunt
> castigantque moras, opere omnis semita fervet.

(Aen. 4.401-407)

In the ant simile, Virgil combines characteristics of other small animals in the *Georgics*. *Aeneid* 4.402-403 describes the weevil, while *Geo.* 1.185 describes the ant. Line 403 recalls the significant fact about the mouse and mole in *Geo.* 1.181-183 who carry off goods to a storehouse. The ant who is *inopi metuens senectae* becomes mindful of the winter (*hiemis memores*) in the *Aeneid*.

Line 403 recalls *Geo.* 4.156-157:

> venturaeque hiemis memores aestate laborem
> experiuntur et in medium quaesita reponunt.

The bees' positive work of gathering their grains into a common store in preparation for a long winter contrasts with the hasty sinister work of the ants, plundering their host's land in the *Aeneid*. *Praedam* suggests *Geo.* 2.60 where the sorry cluster of grapes from the untended vine provides a *praeda* for scavenging birds. *Calle angusto* recalls *Geo.* 1.380, *angustum formica terens iter.*[57] *Pars... trudunt* recalls *Geo.* 4.159 (*pars...ponunt fundamina*) again used of the bees storing up food and of their division of labor, thereby recalling at the same time the bee simile of *Aeneid* 1. The word *grandia* in 405 is used in a similar context at *Geo.* 4.26 (*et grandia conice saxa*) and describes the pebbles from the animals' point of view (see also the mouse, *Geo.* 1.181-182). Finally, *opere fervet* recalls *Geo.* 4.169 and *Aen.* 1.436, *fervet opus, redolentque thymo fraglantia mella.*

But the blurring of distinctions between the various vermin is of little importance. We may compare the similes of *Il.* 2.87ff. (bees), 16.259ff. (wasps), and 2.469ff., 16.641 (flies), and *Arg.*

---

[57] This is also found in Aristotle, *H.A.* 9.38, p. 622, b 25.

4.1452ff. (double simile of flies and ants). Let us look at three of these:

> 'Ήΰτε μυιάων ἀδινάων ἔθνεα πολλά,
> αἵ τε κατὰ σταθμὸν ποιμνήϊον ἠλάσκουσιν
> ὥρῃ ἐν εἰαρινῇ, ὅτε τε γλάγος ἄγγεα δεύει,
> τόσσοι ἐπὶ Τρώεσσι κάρη κομόωντες 'Αχαιοὶ
> ἐν πεδίῳ ἵσταντο διαρραῖσαι μεμαῶτες.
>
> (Il. 2.469-473)

> αὐτίκα δὲ σφήκεσσιν ἐοικότες ἐξεχέοντο
> εἰνοδίοις, οὓς παῖδες ἐριδμαίνωσιν ἔθοντες,
> αἰεὶ κερτομέοντες, ὁδῷ ἔπι οἰκί' ἔχοντας,
> νηπίαχοι· ξυνὸν δὲ κακὸν πολέεσσι τιθεῖσι.
> τοὺς δ' εἴ περ παρά τίς τε κιὼν ἄνθρωπος ὁδίτης
> κινήσῃ ἀέκων, οἱ δ' ἄλκιμον ἦτορ ἔχοντες
> πρόσσω πᾶς πέτεται καὶ ἀμύνει οἷσι τέκεσσι.
> τῶν τότε Μυρμιδόνες κραδίην καὶ θυμὸν ἔχοντες
> ἐκ νηῶν ἐχέοντο· βοὴ δ' ἄσβεστος ὀρώρει.
>
> (Il. 16.259-267)

> ὡς δ' ὁπότε στεινὴν περὶ χηραμὸν εἰλίσσονται
> γειομόροι μύρμηκες ὁμιλαδόν, ἢ ὅτε μυῖαι
> ἀμφ' ὀλίγην μέλιτος γλυκεροῦ λίβα πεπτηυῖαι
> ἄπλητον μεμάασιν ἐπήτριμοι· ὡς τότ' ἀολλεῖς
> πετραίῃ Μινύαι περὶ πίδακι δινεύεσκον.
>
> (Arg. 4.1452-1456)

As can be seen, these pests have their own proper activities and the men have theirs. As Klingner [58] has pointed out, these creatures do not behave as warriors or heroes, only as animals.

But Virgil goes beyond this. The first two lines of his simile are straightforward and traditional. But he then neglects the formal comparee [59] (Klingner's "Wie-Satz") to compare something different, the human behavior of the ants. In other words, his point is not simply to compare ants with heroes, but to create a second comparison of men and ants *within* the simile, emphasizing the military behavior common to both groups.

To do this, Virgil combines elements from his other descriptions of communities of animals. He then adds human details (*umeris, populant, tectoque reponunt,*[60] and *praedam convectant.*[61])

---

[58] Klingner, 450.

[59] Sparrow notes this lack of an apodosis and considers it a sign of incompleteness (32-33).

[60] "Primarily of human structures", *Publi Vergili Maronis Aeneidos Liber Quartus*, ed. A. S. Pease, Cambridge, Mass., 1935, 342.

[61] As the soldiers will actually do in *Aen.* 7.749, 9.613.

The most significant line is 404, *it nigrum campis agmen* which, according to Servius, comes from Ennius (*de elephantis dictum*) and Accius (*de Indis*).[62] Some have considered it "the classic example of Virgil's disregard for the original application of an Ennian phrase," [63] with "an almost comic effect," [64] the whole passage showing Virgil's "secret smile." [65] But there can be no doubt that Virgil is *not* smiling at the Trojan activity. The stately spondees of 404 and 405,[66] the ictus-accent clash, the sinister words *nigrum* (a color after all better suited to ants than elephants), *praedam*, *obnixae*, coupled with the military terms *agmen, agmina cogunt*,[67] combine to give the ants a truly menacing and ominous aspect as has been seen in the *Georgics* and as will be seen in the *Aeneid*.

Even more significant than Virgil's alteration of his sources is his use of the simile in its passage. Clearly, Virgil chose tiny creatures foı this comparison, not only as a link to other similes in the poem, but also to let us see the Trojans as Dido does. For the most un-usual effect of the simile comes *after* its climactic buildup, when the poet suddenly turns and addresses Dido herself, *quis tibi tum, Dido, cernenti talia sensus*. We realize then that we have been prepared by Virgil not only to see the Trojans as ants through his eyes, but in fact through Dido's eyes, just as the Carthaginians had appeared like bees in Book 1 to the eyes of Aeneas. We see then that the point of the simile is to enrich our understanding not of the Trojans but of Dido: Her final, bitter perception of the men with whom she had shared her kingdom as a destructive pack of ants, is contrasted with Aeneas' first perception of the Carthaginians as hardy, constructive bees.[68]

---

[62] Servius says it may come from Accius also, referring to Indians (fr. 26 Mo). Regel and Norden take the line to be typical of Virgil's disregard for the original context from which he borrowed his lines, but Klingner regards the whole passage as appropriately Ennian. For sources and discussion, see Wigodsky, 53 and n. 263.

[63] Wigodsky, 53.

[64] Pease, 342.

[65] Austin, IV, 125.

[66] Both lines have identical rhythms.

[67] For the military aspects of bees, see *Geo.* 4.67-68, 82-83.

[68] Sparrow notices that each time Virgil introduces a simile by *ac veluti* (with the exception of *Aen.* 2.626), an apodosis that describes the scene has preceded it. The lack of such an apodosis here, he says, is a sign of incomplete-ness (32-33). Mackail (*Virgil. The Aeneid*, ed. by J. W. Mackail, Oxford, 1930, 149) also notes "the feebleness of line 412, the awkward repetition of *cogis...cogitur* and the absence of any introductory line to the speech which

There is, of course, nothing like this in the *Georgics*, but we can see that the humanizing details, the particular elements chosen from earlier writers, and the placement of the simile in its passage are all derived from techniques first employed in that poem.

## 2. *Birds*

Descriptions or comparisons involving birds are given a deeply sympathetic coloring in the *Georgics*, but they do not form an extended motif in the *Aeneid*.

The behavior of certain birds and other animals is one of the storm-signs of *Geo.* 1.373-423, a passage adapted from Aratus, with Ciceronian, Lucretian, and other elements added.[69] Each animal described (cow, frog, ant, etc.) is given a unique detail to elevate it above the simple, rambling description of Aratus.

The passage is structured in order that the single characteristics of each species become gradually more human,[70] ending with the final description of the crows. The cranes flee (*fugere*-375); the swallow twitters and plays about the pools (*arguta...circumvolitavit*-376); the rooks are arrayed in ranks like an army (380-381);[71] the sea-birds gambol in the meadows (383-387).[72] Their frolic is set off by the mock-stateliness of the caitiff raven calling down the rain [73] and promenading in stately alliterative spondees (*sola insiccum secum spatiatur*-389). The halcyons try to catch the warm sun in their wings (398-399) and the owl keeps watch at sunset, *vainly* plying her song.[74] Finally, the crows are described in the most human and sympathetic terms:

---

follows, 11.416-436". But, like *Aen.* 2.626, Virgil is not stressing details of scene, but how they appear to us first and then, in a dramatic contrast, how they appear to Dido.

[69] *Phaen.* 932-979, *de Div.* 1.8.14, *D.R.N.* 5.1083 and 410. In addition to making the birds ravens from Aratus' crows, Virgil adds to the description Cicero's moral word *improba*, in 388, and the description of the promenade. On the sources of this passage and Virgil's use of them, see G. Williams, 255-260.

[70] "The charm of Virgil's description consists largely in the way he speaks of birds as though they were human beings". T. E. Page, *P. Vergili Maronis Bucolica et Georgica*, London, 1898, 232.

[71] *Agmine magno, exercitus, densis alis.* See Huxley, 115.

[72] This description seems to come from *Il.* 2.459-469 where Homer mentions the geese, cranes and swans of Cayster. "Latin poets tend to mention swans only". (Huxley, ibid).

[73] In a formula derived from religious ritual.

[74] All this is interwoven with mythological references to bird-metamorphoses (Ceyx-Alcyone, Nisus, Scylla). This is a much-questioned passage, see Richter, 171-172.

Tum liquidas corvi presso ter gutture voces
aut quater ingeminant, et saepe cubilibus altis
nescio qua praeter solitum dulcedine laeti
inter se in foliis strepitant; iuvat imbribus actis
progeniem parvam dulcisque revisere nidos;

(Geo. 1.410-414)

In their fear for their nests, the crows cry (ingeminant) repeatedly [75]
with constricted throats (contrasted with plena voce in 388), and
either chatter or flutter their wings, gladdened despite the impending storm for the chance to rest in their beds (cubilibus) at evening.[76]
The fear is dramatically dispelled by the sharp break in 413 followed by the alliterative iuvat imbribus, the joy that the storm has
spared their little nestlings.[77]

This passage contains two principal features of the previous
passages: 1) the humanizing of the non-human, and 2) the structur-
ings of a paragraph in a climactic fashion to lead up to a thematic
statement. From brief mentions of birds performing human activities (gamboling, arraying like soldiers, talking like priests) to the
mention of birds who had once been humans (halcyons and owls)
to the longer description in plainly human terms, the passage builds
to its Ausklang.

The final harmony of nature depicted in 422-423 completes the
picture of joy suffused through all creatures at the coming of the
storm, Jove's power and governance, and the eternal promise of
his protection.[78]

Clamorem ad sidera tollunt

Dardanidae e muris, spes addita suscitat iras,
tela manu iaciunt, quales sub nubibus atris
Strymoniae dant signa grues atque aethera tranant
cum sonitu fugiuntque Notos clamore secundo.

(Aen. 10.262-266)

Here, the rising shouts of the Trojans are compared to the sound
of the birds, the shower of arrows to their physical appearance.[79]

---

[75] Perhaps in vain, to judge by other uses of ter...quater. See Pease, 471.

[76] The notion implicit in this word is that they "lie down" to sleep
whether they do so in beds or not.

[77] 412 and 414 recur in Geo. 4.55-56; the bees' behavior.

[78] Otis finds these lines an assimilation "of all his subject matter...
to a common feeling-tone that seems...to cover the enormous gap between
owls and crows, on the one hand, and Roman history—the civil wars,
Octavian—on the other". (Otis, 387-388).

[79] Fugere is the only common word besides grues.

The simile depends for its effect upon the visualization of the cry and the straining forward of the birds.[80] The militaristic note of the *Georgics* passage returns in the phrase *dant signa*, with its double meaning of portending destruction and beginning a battle.

The militaristic cranes are found in *Il.* 3.2-6:

Τρῶες μὲν κλαγγῇ τ' ἐνοπῇ τ' ἴσαν, ὄρνιθες ὥς,
ἠΰτε περ κλαγγὴ γεράνων πέλει οὐρανόθι πρό,
αἵ τ' ἐπεὶ οὖν χειμῶνα φύγον καὶ ἀθέσφατον ὄμβρον,
κλαγγῇ ταί γε πέτονται ἐπ' Ὠκεανοῖο ῥοάων,
ἀνδράσι Πυγμαίοισι φόνον καὶ κῆρα φέρουσαι·

This simile is unusual for Homer in that both the object and the subject of the comparison are engaged in identical action, bringing battle. The force of the simile comes from the repeated κλαγγή of the Trojans, contrasted with the σιγή (line 8) of the Greeks.

Virgil has then taken Homer's simile, used it again to describe the Trojans advancing to battle, but has shifted the sense from an auditory to a visual one.

In *Aen.* 4.253-255, Mercury is described:

hinc toto praeceps se corpore ad undas
misit avi similis, quae circum litora, circum
piscosos scopulos humilis volat aequora iuxta:

The repeated use of *circum* echoes *circumvolitavit* in *Geo.* 1.377 and *piscosos* carries the same playful connotation. The comparison is standard epic.[81]

A more emotional coloring is given to the nightingale simile in *Geo.* 4.511-515:

(Orpheus flevit)
qualis populea maerens philomela sub umbra
amissos queritur fetus, quos durus arator
observans nido inplumis detraxit; at illa
flet noctem ramoque sedens miserabile carmen
integrat et maestis late loca questibus implet.

The simile recalls *Od.* 16.216-218 and 19.518-529, in which vultures wail for their lost brood and the nightingale laments Iris. Virgil gives an interesting twist to the allusion. The former describes

---

[80] See K. Quinn, *Virgil's Aeneid: A Critical Description*, Ann Arbor 1968, 434-435.

[81] See *Il.* 15.237-238 (Apollo), *Od.* 1.320 (Athena), 5.52-54 (Hermes), 22.240 (Athena), *Arg.* 4.966-967. No source can be cited with assurance.

Telemachus and Odysseus weeping at their reunion, the latter is Penelope's self-comparison before her yet unrecognized husband, with whom she is already reunited, without knowing it. The *Georgics* simile describes the grief of Orpheus who can never be rejoined with Eurydice.

The style of the passage shows Virgil's special sensitivity in the words *queritur* (512) and *questibus* (515), proper words of mournful elegy; v. 513, laden with grave spondees and heavy elision (*nido implumis*), conveys the harsh wrenching of the nestlings from their home. The mother weeps with a *miserabile carmen* in 515, and "fills the air with griefs far and wide," as does Euryalus' grieving mother in *Aen.* 9.480.

The effect of this simile is best seen in the context of the entire passage,[82] but I believe we can see, in the irrational victimization of the little bird compared to the fabled tragedy of the mythical Orpheus, Virgil's unique sympathy for all creatures great and small.[83]

By and large, bird similes in the *Aeneid* are rather conventional. They most often strike a single point of comparison, such as sound or speed.[84] Birds of prey are used three times, and twice birds are killed.[85] With the exception of the cranes fleeing before the storm, only one can be traced to the *Georgics*,[86] and in this, the birds are an impersonal swarm, more like bees than birds.

But two similes stand out: the comparison of Hecuba and the Trojan women cowering about the altar like doves (2.515-517) and Juturna flitting about like a black swift (12.468-480). These do not bear an essential relationship to any descriptions in the *Georgics* but do share with them a highly empathetic quality.

---

[82] See Otis' discussion, 201-202.

[83] Wilkinson compares *Geo.* 2.208-211 (the birds dispossessed by warfare) and remarks, "Who save Virgil, contemplating the felling of trees to realise timber long idle and release land especially suitable for corn-growing, would have spared a thought for the birds stranded in mid-air with their ancient 'homes' gone?" (126-127).

[84] Noise of weapons = din of cranes in 10.262-266, *clamor* of Latins = various birds in 11.447-458, noise of swans = men singing of leader in 7.699-705, speed of Mercury = speed of bird, 4.252-255, speed of Mnestheus' ship = speed of bird in 5.213-219.

[85] Turnus (eagle) kills Lycus (swan) in 9.556-566; Camilla (hawk) kills Ligus (dove) in 11.715-724; and Tarchon is like an eagle clutching a snake in 11.751-758.

[86] The souls compared to birds at *Aen.* 6.305-314.

Hecuba and her daughters are taking shelter from the figurative storm that is destroying Troy:

> Hic Hecuba et natae nequiquam altaria circum,
> praecipites atra ceu tempestate columbae,
> condensae et divom amplexae simulacra sedebant.

> *(Aen. 2.515-517)*

The expressiveness of the simile resides mostly in its style. The birds fall swiftly (*praecipites*) after which the impending storm is described in heavy spondees. Ictus and accent clash reflects the violence that threatens them in 516. The similes are intensified by the characteristic vulnerability of the doves,[87] coupled with their passivity and mutual affection. This pathetic quality will be recalled in the description of the dove tied to a tether in the archery contest at 5.485-518.[88]

At 12.473-478, Juturna in battle is described:

> Nigra velut magnas domini cum divitis aedes
> pervolat et pinnis alta atria lustrat hirundo
> pabula parva legens nidisque loquacibus escas
> et nunc porticibus vacuis, nunc umida circum
> stagna sonat: similis medios Iuturna per hostis
> fertur equis rapidoque volans obit omnia curru

Turnus' position has now so deteriorated that his sister can only try to preserve him like a maternal swallow, scrounging scraps from a stately mansion to feed her starving fledglings. Putnam aptly compares the death of Polites in 2.526-530 and shows the "mood of impending disaster" evident here.[89] In addition, the previous simile of Hecuba, another pathetic mother figure, links this simile with the fall of Troy. In addition, Juturna is compared to a *black* swallow, an ominous, fearful aspect of her otherwise

---

[87] Doves are the most frequently victimized birds. See the "sources" of this simile, *Il.* 21.493f., Aesch. *Suppl.* 223f., and Eur. *Androm.* 1140f.

[88] This pathetic quality seems lacking in *Aen.* 5.213-219, in which Mnestheus' ship moves through the water like a flushed dove through the air. The echo appears to be Apollonius' comparison of the Argo to a hawk (2.932-935) but, as G. Williams points out (668), Virgil uses the simile simply as a more appropriate image to describe the motion of the ship (the dove now claps his wings furiously, now he glides, just as the oarmen row madly, then cruise). On *volvere*, see Perkins, 270.

[89] Putnam, 173.

sympathetic description.[90] She is pathetic in her actions and ominous in her appearance because thanks to Venus she knows the truth of Turnus' doom. This makes the description of her futile activity more dramatic, even more tragic than any simile save the nightingale in the *Georgics*. The comparison itself may not be original, but clearly the subjective flavor is Virgil's own.[91]

While these bird similes do not have *direct* sources in the *Georgics*, this limited discussion may show that Virgil's sympathetic treatment of birds is quite similar throughout. The two instances which have only the slightest relationship with other sources, share an emotional sensitivity and structural significance clearly displayed in the *Georgics* as a whole.

### 3. Snakes

B. M. W. Knox appends to his famous article on serpent imagery in *Aeneid* 2 only a few remarks on the indebtedness of this intricate patterning to the few lines in the *Georgics* devoted to snakes.[92] After citing the significant verbal parallels, he says:

> This is clearly a passage (*Geo.* 3.414-439) which was often present in Virgil's mind as he wrote the second book of the *Aeneid*; its presence there may be connected with the dominance which the image of the serpent assumed. More than this can hardly be suggested, for in the complexity of a great poet's imagery we must recognize a mystery which lies beyond the frontiers of conscious art.[93]

Perhaps this is true. But it is possible to go beyond Knox's brief mention to show that 1) the *Georgics* catalogue, brief as it is, shows the two chief characteristics of snakes used in the *Aeneid*: a) their ability to cause sudden terror for which, Knox says, "Virgil

---

[90] On the ornithologically "inept" description of the sparrow, see J. N. Hough, "Bird-Imagery in Roman Poetry" *CJ* 70 (1974), p. 7.

[91] Conington-Nettleship say the simile is original with Virgil (*ad Aen.* 12.473, 447, but cf. Theocr. 14.39-40 and *Od.* 22.240. Juturna's behavior recalls the boat-race at *Aen.* 5.142-150. However, the Roman elements (the garden and the aviary) together with the echoes of *Aen.* 6.310-311 and the *inania regna* of 6.629 seem original. See A. J. McKay's review of Hornsby, *AJP* 94 (1973), 317. On the lack of verbal correspondence in the simile, see Perkins, 268.

[92] B. M. W. Knox, "The Serpent and the Flame: The Imagery of the Second Book of the *Aeneid*", *AJP* 71 (1950), 379-400.

[93] Ibid., 399-400.

had good precedent in the Latin tradition" [94] and b) their habit of rejuvenation by sloughing their skin, for which there seems less of a tradition; 2) in humanizing the snake, Virgil lays a basis for the application of serpentine characteristics to men of both sides in the fall of Troy; and 3) much of his description in *Aeneid* 2 is a direct result of his conception of the snake in the *Georgics* and does not come from any one Greek source.

nec rapit immensos orbis per humum neque tanto
squameus in spiram tractu se colligit anguis.

(*Geo.* 2.153-154)

Saepe sub immotis praesepibus aut mala tactu
vipera delituit caelumque exterrita fugit
aut tecto adsuetus coluber succedere et umbrae
(pestis acerba boum) pecorique aspergere virus
fovit humum. Cape saxa manu, cape robora, pastor,
tollentemque minas et sibila colla tumentem
deice! Iamque fuga timidum caput abdidit alte,
cum medii nexus extremaeque agmina caudae
solvontur tardosque trahit sinus ultimus orbis.

(*Geo.* 3.416-424)

Est etiam ille malus Calabris in saltibus anguis
squamea convolvens sublato corpore terga
atque notis longam maculosus grandibus alvom,
qui, dum amnes ulli rumpuntur fontibus et dum
vere madent udo terrae ac pluvialibus Austris,
stagna colit ripisque habitans hic piscibus atram
improbus ingluviem ranisque loquacibus explet;
postquam exusta palus terraeque ardore dehiscunt,
exsilit in siccum et flammantia lumina torquens
saevit agris asperque siti atque exterritus aestu.
Nec mihi tum mollis sub divo carpere somnos
neu dorso nemoris libeat iacuisse per herbas,
cum positis novus exuviis nitidusque iuventa
volvitur, aut catulos tectis aut ova relinquens,
arduus ad solem et linguis micat ore trisulcis.

(*Geo.* 3.425-439)

Inprovisum aspris veluti qui sentibus anguem
pressit humi nitens trepidusque repente refugit
attollentem iras et caerula colla tumentem:
haut secus Androgeos visu tremefactus abibat.

(*Aen.* 2.379-382)

---

[94] Ibid., 379.

qualis ubi in lucem coluber mala gramina pastus,
frigida sub terra tumidum quem bruma tegebat,
nunc, positis novus exuviis nitidusque iuventa,
lubrica convolvit sublato pectore terga
arduos ad solem et linguis micat ore trisulcis.

*(Aen.* 2.471-475)

Qualis saepe viae deprensus in aggere serpens,
aerea quem oblicum rota transiit aut gravis ictu
seminecem liquit saxo lacerumque viator;
nequiquam longos fugiens dat corpore tortus
parte ferox ardensque oculis et sibila colla
arduus attollens; pars volnere clauda retentat
nexantem nodis seque in sua membra plicantem:
tali remigio navis se tarda movebat;

*(Aen.* 5.273-280)

The second and third passages form one paragraph in a longer
section of Book 3 (384-469) that builds up images of the cruelty
and terror in nature (from thistles and briars to robbers, to snakes,
to diseases), climaxing with the extended description of the plague
at Noricum. This theme is clear in the snake passage and it will
inform the similes of the snakes in the *Aeneid*.

The passage begins with the viper who attacks only the herds
and whom the shepherd can kill with his sticks and stones. The
snake is deadly (*mala tactu*) but also frightened (*exterrita*). Wounded,
and probably dying, he buries his frightened head (*timidum caput*)
and pathetic, crawls away.

The Calabrian serpent is entirely different. It represents real
evil, sudden, terrible, and fatal. Virgil piles up the images of the
parched land and frenzied thirst, adding his note of personal fear,
after which he clinches the paragraph with the embodiment of his
theme: the horrible menace of the snake on the prowl.

In the *Aeneid*, the snakes first appear at the execution of the
fate of Laocoön and his sons (2.199-227). The principal difference
between these serpents and those in the *Georgics*, apart from their
being sea-snakes, is the fact of their great size. But there are nevertheless parallels: They come from the quiet sea (*tranquilla per
alta* [95]); Virgil prays the Calabrian serpent will not attack him

---

[95] Virgil does not elsewhere use an epithet with *altus*, reinforcing in this
case, the peacefulness of the sea, intensifying the shock of the unanticipated
snakes.

sleeping under the open sky (*sub divo-Geo.* 3.435), both passages emphasizing the unexpected disruption of tranquillity by the snake. The snakes tower over the waves (*superant undas-Aen.* 2.207) or reach up to the sun (*arduus ad solem-Geo.* 3.439); their large backs writhe with coils (*sinuatque immensa volumine terga-*2.208, *immensos orbis-Geo.* 2.153); their eyes flash fire (*ardentisque oculos-*2.210, *flammantia lumina-Geo.* 3.433); they hiss (*sibila* (of the mouth)-*Aen.* 2.211, (of the neck)-*Geo.* 3.421) and their tongues flicker (*lambebant linguis vibrantibus ora-Aen.* 2.211, *linguis micat ore trisulcis-Geo.* 3.439); they move their tails in a coil, but like a military line line (*agmine certo-Aen.* 2.212, *agmina caudae-Geo.* 3.423). Laocoön vainly tries to defend himself with a spear (*auxilio subeuntem ac tela ferentem-Aen.* 2.216) as the farmer had successfully defended himself with staves (*robora-Geo.* 3.420); the snakes again tower over their victim as in the *Georgics* and strike (*corripiunt spirisque ligant ingentibus-Aen.* 2.217, *nec rapit immensos orbis per humum neque tanto/squameus in spiram tractu se colligit anguis-Geo.* 2.153-154). Having encountered man, they flee (*effugiunt-Aen.* 2.226, *fuga-Geo.* 3.422). The viper in the *Georgics* comes from beneath a shed (416); the snakes go beneath a statue after their murders are committed (2.227).

As in other passages, when Virgil says nearly the same thing he almost always varies his vocabulary.[96] But as he varies his vocabulary in describing the same things, he repeats vocabulary in describing *different* things (e.g. humans and abstractions) and this is unique. This practice depends very much upon the initial identification of these real snakes as symbols of sudden terror and quick destruction, in a style and context very similar to that of the *Georgics*. We are therefore prepared to associate fear with the very movement of the snakes when we are told the reaction of the Trojans to Laocoön's death, *insinuat pavor* (229).

The Trojans bring the horse in through the walls of Troy, *pedibus rotarum/subiciunt lapsus* (235-236). *Labi* is, as Knox points out, one of the key "snake words," [97] but curiously enough, it does not appear in any of the snake descriptions in the *Georgics*, only in the snake constellation at *Geo.* 1.244. Its particular sense of "glide"

---

[96] E.g. *ardentis oculis: flammantia lumina*; *lambebant linguis: linguis micat.*
[97] Knox, 379 and n. 2.

extended to "slither" is also used of horses in *Geo.* 3.180 and *Aen.* 1.147 (both referring to the speed of chariots). The use of the word in 236 recalls 226 where it described a serpent. Knox says, "The metaphor is surprising, if not grotesque: a horse is not much like a serpent." [98] Maybe so, but a passage in the *Georgics* shows that the metaphor may not be so surprising.

At *Aen.* 2.208, the sea-snakes' bodies skim the main *sinuatque immensa volumine terga*. The four-year-old horse, itching for the arena, strong but unpredictable (cf. the breaking process at *Geo.* 3.205-208) is said to "bend his legs in alternating curves" (*sinuetque alterna volumina crurum-Geo.* 3.192). The verbal association is clear.[99]

When the Greeks attack, the Trojans have all fallen into a deep sleep (253) which one associates with the sleep Virgil prays may not fall upon him at *Geo.* 3.435-436, lest the snake attack him. This sleep is particularly important in conjunction with the snake because, at the moment of attack, as Knox says, "The principal instruments of the Trojan downfall, the Trojan fear, the horse, the Greek fleet, the deep sleep, the fire, have all now been linked with the image of the serpent." [100] Sinon himself echoes *sinuo* in his name, the verb recurs in his story, and in 2.136, the prose word *delitui* describes him as it had the snake in *Geo.* 3.417.

The simile of Androgeos (fourth quoted passage above) has been well-prepared for. Its source is *Il.* 3.33-37:

ὡς δ' ὅτε τίς τε δράκοντα ἰδὼν παλίνορσος ἀπέστη
οὔρεος ἐν βήσσῃς, ὑπό τε τρόμος ἔλλαβε γυῖα,
ἂψ δ' ἀνεχώρησεν, ὦχρός τέ μιν εἷλε παρειάς,
ὡς αὖτις καθ' ὅμιλον ἔδυ Τρώων ἀγερώχων
δείσας Ἀτρέος υἱὸν Ἀλέξανδρος θεοειδής.

---

[98] Ibid., 386.

[99] The verb *sinuo* is Virgil's invention. (See Austin, II, 103-104). The horse-snake correlation has been established in advance of *Aen.* 2.205. Since it is difficult to think of these two animals as alike, we are left to conclude that Virgil uses the verb *sinuo* to describe not the habit of the snake, but anything that represents the potential for sudden violence. Similarly, when the horse is described as *arduus armatos mediis in moenibus adstans*, we are reminded of *arduus ad solem et linguis micat ore trisulcis* in the simile comparing Pyrrhus to a snake and the description of the Calabrian serpent in *Geo.* 3.439. Another curious correlation is that the boat-race in Book 5 begins with a simile comparing the barques to horses and ends comparing a vessel to a snake. For *arduus* of a horse in the *Georgics*, see 2.145, 3.79.

[100] Knox, 390.

Homer describes the terror but not the snake in the simile, while Virgil describes the hissing and coiling of the snake in the simile and the terror in the narrative as well.[101] Aeneas the snake is, by his own admission, temporarily insane (348ff.), and he has the full sudden violence of the snake. As Androgeos has become a Laocoön, so Aeneas has become a Sinon.[102]

But Aeneas' *dolus* betrays him. He and his men, in the stolen Greek armor, are found out and his attempt at defense fails. As Knox says, "His brief assumption of the characteristics of the serpent is revealed...as a pathetic masquerade; the real serpent is at the gates of Priam's palace." [103]

The main point of the many snake associations of Pyrrhus (see 48off., 552, 663) is that he represents *patent* violence. The serpent, as a figure in this book, is no longer the lurking deceitful viper but is now the overt symbol of open ferocity.

The simile of 471-475 draws on *Il.* 22.93-97: [104]

ὡς δὲ δράκων ἐπὶ χειῇ ὀρέστερος ἄνδρα μένῃσι,
βεβρωκὼς κακὰ φάρμακ', ἔδυ δέ τέ μιν χόλος αἰνός,
σμερδαλέον δὲ δέδορκεν ἑλισσόμενος περὶ χειῇ·
ὡς Ἕκτωρ ἄσβεστον ἔχων μένος οὐχ ὑπεχώρει,
πύργῳ ἔπι προὔχοντι φαεινὴν ἀσπίδ' ἐρείσας·

Virgil's primary addition is to bring out the fear of both man *and* snake. He also contrasts the darkness from which the snake comes (*Aen.* 2.472) with its gleaming aspect (473). Both the youth and the patina are in the *Georgics* (3.437), as is the motion of the back (*Geo.* 3.426: *Aen.* 2.474). The Calabrian serpent, the most fearful of the snakes, who preys on sleeping victims and is depicted as mad (*improbus*-431, *saevit, asper, exterritus*-434), is recalled by the simile of Pyrrhus who commits the most terrible crimes in a mad (*furentem*-499) passion.[105] The shedding of the skin may well

---

[101] The elements added to Homer's description come largely from the *Georgics*. In both passages, the sound of the snake is heard in the hissing "s" sounds (*adsuetus coluber succedere, improvisum aspris*) and the description of *Aen.* 2.381 is a near repeat from *Geo.* 3.241, except that *iras* is added, perhaps reflecting χόλος in *Il.* 22.94 and *caerula* is added for *sibila* perhaps from the description of the snake in *Geo.* 4.482. The dark-blue quality may be due to the nocturnal occasion of the scene.

[102] Knox, 391.

[103] Ibid., 392.

[104] See also Nicander, *Ther.* 31ff., the snake haughty after sloughing its skin.

[105] See also *Geo.* 2.153-154 and *Aen.* 2.217.

represent Pyrrhus as a new Achilles, but it equally shows the new dimension of the snake, the open symbol of fatal violence.

There are two more significant reminiscences of the *Georgics* in this book.

Aeneas describes Helen: [106]

limina Vestae
servantem et tacitam secreta in sede latentem...

*(Aen.* 2.567-568)

This recalls the lurking snake *(servantem ripas-Geo.* 4.459) which killed Eurydice, while Helen's seclusion at 574 *(abdiderat sese)* recalls the *coluber* which *timidum caput abdidit alte* in *Geo.* 3.422. The former simply describes a common characteristic of the latter, but the empathetic picture in the latter example of the snake burying its *frightened* head certainly applies to the timorous *(praemetuens*-573) Helen. She is thus like the helpless frightened viper which, no longer capable of arousing fear or violence in men, can only cower in fear.

Knox outlines the serpent reminiscences in the description of the flame on Ascanius' head in 682-687. The only real reminiscence of the *Georgics* is the phrase *tactuque innoxia* which reverses the *mala tactu* of the viper in *Geo.* 3.416.

We have seen in *Aeneid* 2 the development of the serpent image from one of concealment and deceit (Sinon, the horse) to one of sudden terror striking from concealment (the serpents from Tenedos, Aeneas) to open violence (Pyrrhus),[107] and finally to a positive portent much like that of the serpent at Anchises' tomb in Book 5. This follows the order of the snakes in the earlier "catalogue" of *Geo.* 3.414-439, and nearly every characteristic of the snake in *Aeneid* 2 occurs in the *Georgics*.[108]

The most important point I would like to stress, however, is that the special qualities of the snakes in the *Georgics*, their capacity for fear, madness, anger, etc. are the most important characteristics Virgil notes. The viper threatens *(tollentem minas)* and Aeneas rages *(attollentem iras)*, the wounded viper is *timidus*, Helen is

---

[106] On the uncertainty of the Helen Episode, see ch. 3, p. 101, n. 5 +6.

[107] This differs slightly from Knox's conclusions (397-398), but is in essential agreement.

[108] The flame and serpent imagery combined is foreshadowed in the *Georgics*, with Calabrian serpent's *flammantia lumina.*

*praementuens*, the serpent is *improbus* and *asper*, Pyrrhus rages madly (*furentem*). All I mean to show is that the snakes in the *Georgics* (in the descriptions that give them human qualities) prepare for the men in the *Aeneid* who are given particular snake-like qualities (e.g. Sinon lurks like a snake-*delitui*) and that this blurring of the distinction between man and animal raises the significance of the symbol to an abstract level not found in earlier authors.[109]

### 4. Bees

In Book Four of the *Georgics*, the proportions of practical discussion of the bees and mythological narrative (excepting the proem and the digression on the Corycian old man) are nearly equal (276 lines of the former, 243 of the latter). The reason for this emphasis on the mythological as well as the practical is found in the famously ambiguous words of the proem:

> Admiranda tibi levium spectacula rerum
> magnanimosque duces totiusque ordine gentis
> mores et studia et populos et proelia dicam.
> In tenui labor; at tenuis non gloria, si quem
> numina laeva sinunt auditque vocatus Apollo.
>
> *(Geo.* 4.3-7)

With the exception of the word *tenuis*, these lines might well begin the *Aeneid*. Ostensibly, the bees are to be treated as no other animal in the poem, by virtue of their divine as well as human characteristics. Virgil will show not only the proper pursuits (the *labor*), but the results (the *gloria*) of the work, as he exemplifies piety in the *Aeneid*, not in the didactic manner of Cato and Varro, but *descriptively*, injecting his original and personal conception of the bee-community into the narrative.

The mythology of the Aristaeus episode will then associate the perfect society with its divine origins (*naturas apibus quas Iuppiter ipse/addidit*) and contrast individual man's passions and mortality with the asexual and deathless bee-community. This Virgil does by comparing the relationship of men and gods with that of the human and divine elements within the bees themselves.

The human and divine relation to the bees is alternately stressed throughout the book: lines 8-15, *man* in control of the bees, setting

---

[109] The two sources quoted are the only snake similes in Homer.

up a hive, insuring a peaceful settlement; 149-238-*Jove* gave them certain characteristics; 239-280-*man* controls the life of the bees once they have settled in the hive, gathering the honey, protecting them from a harsh winter and disease; 281-314-*divine* spontaneous generation from a dead ox. Following this alternately arranged (abab) half of the book, human and divine are united in the figure of *deus Aristaeus*.

Through care and observation of the bees man somehow becomes associated with the divine.[110] And likewise, Virgil associates the bees with men by humanizing their behavior. I shall mention briefly the details of this humanization and their parallels in the *Aeneid*.

The bees have a settled home (*Principio sedes apibus statioque petenda*). The hive is described in terms of a Roman house: [111] it is the *sedes augusta* (228) or *aedes* (258) of a *rex* (75, 106, 201, 212), has a *lar* (43) and *penates* (155). It is described as a *domus* (133, 159) having *tecta* (104, 153, 187, 256), *limina* (188, 257), *portae* (78, 165, 185), *fores* (247), *thalami* (189), *cubilia* (243), and *thesauri* (229) in *regna* (202). Its *quirites* (201) have a *patria* (155) with *oppida* (178), *castra* (108), and an *urbs* (154) with *moenia* (193). The hive is the best place for bees, but they may also live *effosis... latebris/sub terra fovere larem, penitusque repertae/pumicibusque cavis exesaeque arboris antro* (42-44). The importance of their hive will be discussed later.

Once established in the hive, they begin their natural task immediately, *nescio qua dulcedine laetae*. They swarm toward heaven and return home to nestle *intima cunabula*. Bees can not only taste (61-62) and smell (62-63) but also hear (64).

The bees are most human, indeed most like characters in the *Aeneid* when they do battle as a result of rivalry between two kings (67-87). They tremble with the spirit of war (*trepidantia bello* (69), see *Aen.* 7.482), ready their arms (*aptant*, see 2.672, 11.8), fight on an open field (*camposque patentis*, see 5.552) with their wings glittering (see *pueri lucent*, 5.553-554). The chiefs are in the middle (5.330), some drones will flee when defeated (*hos aut hos* (84-85) are persuaded to fight in 10.9-10), and the great strife can be

---

[110] In the same way, care for the fields and observation of the skies in *Georgics* 1 insure peace with Jupiter.

[111] It is *seu corticibus tibi suta cavatis/seu lento fuerint alvaria vimine texta* (cf. the description of the House of Romulus, *Aen.* 8.654).

dispelled with a handful of dust (cf. the flight of the Rutulians amid a cloud of dust, 12.463).

When the battle is over, the victor glows *squalentibus maculis* (defeated men gleam with gold in the *Aeneid*, cf. Theron in 10.314 and Bitias in 9.707).

In their *urbs*, they pass their lives (*agitant aevum*, (154), see *Aen.* 10.235), some work in the fields, some in the houses (for division of labor in general, see *Aen.* 1.442, 2.332, 7.163, 11.882), and some are sentries (9.174-175). They glow with work (4.407), like the Cyclopes working with the panting bellows (170-175: *Aen.* 8.449-453). They are inspired with a passion for gain, work hard, eat dinner, and return to work on their houses before night comes (169-190).

So far, the descriptions of the habits of the bees have parallels in the behavior of men, gods and divine men (especially Aeneas) in the *Aeneid*. But in lines 197-209, Virgil is careful to point out that the bees are different from men in that they do not bear children as man does but they rather bear them home from the flowers in which they find them, carrying them in their mouths (200-201). Love would be an indulgence, sex an enervation and birth a toil, all of which would distract the bees from their work and deplete their energy.[112] It is as if Jove has given them this freedom from love and birth so that they might work as hard as they possibly can all their lives. So hard do they work, in fact, that often a worker will expire on the job (203-205); yet, though the individual die, the race continues immortal (206-210).

The implied comparison of the bees and the human race continues in the description of the king and the valiant support his subjects lend him as *pulchramque petunt per vulnera mortem* (218; see also *Aen.* 11.647).

The bees share the divine intelligence and a draught of the heavenly *aether* as Anchises says the soul does in *Aen.* 6.724-727 and therefore the body of no one of them will entirely pass away.

---

[112] Klingner (301-303) finds elements from the Eleusinian mystery-cult in the bees. The priestesses of the cult, called *melissae* by Callimachus, drink from the surface of the water (ἄκρον ἄωτον) as the bees drink *summa flumina* (54-55). The celibacy of the priestesses and bees may also be compared. On the elements of the mysteries and the character of Proserpina in *Georgics* 1 as well as the relation of Proserpina and Eurydice in Virgil, see P. A. Johnston, "Eurydice and Proserpina in the *Georgics*", *TAPA* 107 (1977), 162 n. 3.

So passionate are they in defense of their hive that they will lay down their lives to protect it (232-233). When their number is depleted, the survivors work all the harder to replenish it and repair their home (248-250).

Virgil is then explicit in the comparison of man to bees when he speaks of diseases and cures (251-280).

At last he describes the marvelous *bugonia*, incidentally introducing the description of the legend (*prima repetens ab origine-* 286) with the words Aeneas uses to introduce himself to Dido (*Aen.* 1.372).

It is striking to notice that the bee-scenes in the *Aeneid* occur in the first and last books of each half of the poem. The bees of 1 and 12 have an established dwelling place, a hive or a cave, while in 6 and 7 they are a homeless swarm. They are seen by Aeneas as a metaphor for man in Books 1 and 6; they are described more objectively in 7 and 12.

> Solae communis natos, consortia tecta
> urbis habent magnisque agitant sub legibus aevom
> et patriam solae et certos novere penatis;
> venturaeque hiemis memores aestate laborem
> experiuntur et in medium quaesita reponunt.
> Namque aliae victu invigilant et foedere pacto
> exercentur agris; pars intra saepta domorum
> narcissi lacrimam et lentum de cortice gluten
> prima favis ponunt fundamina, deinde tenacis
> suspendunt ceras; aliae spem gentis adultos
> educunt fetus; aliae purissima mella
> stipant et liquido distendunt nectare cellas.
> Sunt, quibus ad portas cecidit custodia sorti
> inque vicem speculantur aquas et nubila caeli,
> aut onera accipiunt venientum, aut agmine facto
> ignavom fucos pecus a praesepibus arcent:
> fervit opus redolentque thymo fraglantia mella.
>
> (*Geo.* 4.153-169)
>
> Qualis apes aestate nova per florea rura
> exercet sub sole labor, cum gentis adultos
> educunt fetus, aut cum liquentia mella
> stipant et dulci distendunt nectare cellas,
> aut onera accipiunt venientum, aut agmine facto
> ignavum fucos pecus a praesepibus arcent;
> fervet opus redolentque thymo fraglantia mella.
>
> (*Aen.* 1.430-436)
>
> Hunc circum innumerae gentes populique volabant:
> ac veluti in pratis ubi apes aestate serena

6

floribus insidunt variis et candida circum
lilia funduntur, strepit omnis murmure campus.

(*Aen.* 6.706-709)

These passages show three similar descriptions, one involving wholesale repetition, the other retaining only the most significant words (*apes, aestate, floribus*).[113]

In the *Georgics* passage, the humanizing details I have remarked on previously are present, as is the familiar structure. The paragraph is built in three parts: the division of labor in the bee-community builds to a concluding sentence expressing the *natura* of the bees, their happy and enthusiastic work (*fervit opus redolentque thymo fraglantia mella*); this work is then magnified by comparison to the mighty work of the Cyclopes (170-175); a further description of the labor-division balances the first section and, in the final lines, negates the grand simile with the reminder that the bees must ballast themselves with tiny stones when flying.

So in the *Aeneid* the bee-simile climaxes the description of the Carthaginians with the ἐπιφώνημα at 436. The internal arrangement, however, is different. The comparison really begins in line 421 with the word *magalia*, used of beehives.[114] The simile should be keyed by line 423 (*instant ardentes*), the eager work, followed by the division of labor (423-425). But the lines preceding the simile describe the laws and ordination of magistrates and a senate, the digging of harbors and the foundation of a theatre (426-429), tasks which in themselves do not present a ready comparison with bees. The Homeric practice (as in the examples quoted in the discussion of the ant-simile above) would have been to associate the hard-working bees *immediately* with the hard-working men. But Virgil first alludes to the similarity of men and bees, then speaks of human tasks, *then* gives the simile, altering the epic conventions much as he had in the ant-simile. He forces the reader to ask himself in what ways bees resemble man making a government and building public works. The answer involves their selfless devotion to the community, the unique conception of the bee-state set forth in the *Georgics*. Thus it may not be too far afield to say that lines

---

[113] Only four words are altered in *Aen.* 1.431-433 from *Geo.* 4.162-164 and these changes are minimal: *purissima mella* becomes *liquentia mella* but *dulci nectare* becomes *liquido nectare*. *Geo.* 4.167-169 are repeated exactly in *Aen.* 1.434-436.

[114] Also used of Libyan huts in *Geo.* 3.340.

426-429 make explicit this crucial thematic conception of the bees as ideal citizens, a conception which was only implicit in the *Georgics*. In other words, Virgil elaborates his original statement about the bees by his language, his paragraph structure, and his alteration of conventions.

There are, however, significant differences between the two passages. The similes consist of two sentences with *aut...aut... aut* linking the several inverted *cum*-clauses. The narrative in the *Georgics* contains antitheses (*aliae... pars... aliae... pars*) as well as a brief polysyndeton in the repeated section (*aut... aut*) and the absence of subordinate clauses compares more favorably with the simple or compound sentences in the latter, divided into different lengths for variety with more antithesis and polysyndeton.[115]

As significant as what he repeats is what he does not repeat. He omits any mention of the subject of *Geo.* 4.153-157, the rearing of children, the joint ownership of homes, and fidelity to the king. Noticeably absent is a reference to the repulsion of outsiders. Mention of frugality in storing up for the winter is not appropriate either, both because it would violate the carefree summer atmosphere and also because the Carthaginians are building a city, not manufacturing and storing food.

But this does not matter for the moment. One crucial fact about the bees has been left out. The simile shows Aeneas now aware of the harmony possible in a divinely sanctioned political state [116] and this attracts him to stay in Carthage. But the lesson of the *Georgics*, that the accomplishment of this harmony precludes the indulgence in *amor*, is omitted. It is Dido's tragedy that she never learns this,[117] and Virgil never explicitly connects asexuality with the bees in the *Aeneid*, but clearly the intrusion of *amor* corrupts the Carthaginian concord and ruins the scene (literally and figuratively) that Aeneas first sees.

In Book 1, Aeneas speaks to Venus and, in effect, begins his adventure at Carthage with the very words which begin the account of the *bugonia*:

---

[115] See J. Grant, "Dido Melissa", *Phoenix*, 23 (1969), 381-382.

[116] As Jupiter gives his sanction to the founding of Rome in *Aeneid* 1 and 10, so he had rewarded the bees for feeding him honey when he was hiding from his father in the cave at Mt. Dicte. See *Geo.* 4.149-150.

[117] Her dying words mention the construction and reflect on how happy her life would have been if she had never met Aeneas. (651-658).

expediam prima repetens ab origine famam

(Geo. 4.286)

O dea, si prima repetens ab origine pergam

(Aen. 1.372)

Bee associations are rife through the rest of the book, after the simile. The discovery on the beach by the Phoenicians of the skull of the war-horse (441-445) where now bees live, recalls Carthage and recent history.[118] The passionate fighting of the contending kings follows (448-493), in which the women symbolically carry Troilus (his robe) to the Temple of Pallas much as the bees carry back their leader from battle (*Geo.* 4.217-218). Penthesilea in her fury and golden belt (491-493) must appear to shine like the bees. Aeneas, feared dead, is described in 546 as feeding on air (*vescitur aura aetheria*) as does his son in 3.339 and as the bees do in *Geo.* 4.220-221.

As the Trojans prepare to leave Carthage, the ant-simile reverses the happy atmosphere of the bee-simile. There are many verbal parallels not only with the bee-simile but also with the bees and ants of the *Georgics*.[119]

The major thematic parallel with the bee-simile is the contrast of the two proverbial "communities" in nature.[120] Both have strong leaders without whom the society cannot survive and both have ambitions of power and longevity.[121]

Through reminiscences of the *Georgics*, Dido may be seen to reflect the King Bee.[122] In addition, in the simile of the wounded doe (4.69-73), line 72 (*illa fuga silvas saltusque peragrat*) recalls the description of the bees setting out for work in *Geo.* 4.53 (*illae continuo saltus silvasque peragrant*).[123]

It is thus apparent that while *Aeneid* 1 had shown the harmony of the bee-community, just as in the *Georgics*, the cause of this harmony, as expressly stated in the *Georgics*, is not made fully

---

[118] See n. 131 below.

[119] E.g. *agmine facto*, 434. The bees are seen from a hilltop as the ants are seen by Dido from a tower.

[120] For bees and ants associated, see Pliny, *N.H.* 11.108 and Quint. 5.11.24.

[121] Carthage: 444-445; Rome: 278-279.

[122] Grant, 387-388, cites the use of the verb *stipare* used of packing honey in *Geo.* 4.164 and of bees attending the *rex* in 215-216 as in the three times the Tyrians press around Dido (1.496-497, 4.136, 544-545).

[123] See Grant, 389. The Cretan setting is also significant.

known until *Aeneid* 4. The crucial fact about the successful hive is the absence of *amor* (*Geo.* 4.198-199), which every other race (*amor omnibus idem-Geo.* 3.244), including man (*Geo.* 3.245ff.), has. It is this *amor* which prevents Dido from fulfilling her responsibilities as queen and prevents a glorious destiny for Carthage.[124] That *amor* is a *fault* is made clear in the words immediately following the ant-simile, the climax to which the thematic insect-similes have pointed:

> Improbe Amor, quid non mortalia pectora cogis!
> Ire iterum in lacrimas, iterum temptare precando
> cogitur et supplex animos submittere amori,
> ne quid inexpertum frustra moritura relinquat.
>
> (*Aen.* 4.412-415)

As Virgil contrasts the peaceful animals in the countryside with the raging Dido, he uses the phrase *pecudes pictaeque volucres* from *Geo.* 3.243, the same description of love among the animals noted above. She who had virtually renounced love after the death of Sychaeus has now become its victim. Raging like the *hippomanes*-crazed horse, failing in her role as queen, maddened by her unsuccessful submission to love, Dido reflects at once the lesson of the doomed beasts of *Geo.* 3 as Aeneas reflects the lesson of the happy bees of *Geo.* 4.

The simile of Book 6 retains this essential quality of joy and peaceful harmony, but with an almost entirely different wording, perhaps reflecting its Greek sources.

The bee-lily association occurs in Apollonius *Arg.* 1.879-883:

> ὡς δ' ὅτε λείρια καλὰ περιβρομέουσι μέλισσαι
> πέτρης ἐκχύμεναι σιμβληίδος, ἀμφὶ δὲ λειμὼν
> ἐρσήεις γάνυται, ταὶ δὲ γλυκὺν ἄλλοτε ἄλλον
> καρπὸν ἀμέργουσιν πεποτημέναι· ὣς ἄρα ταίγε
> ἐνδυκὲς ἀνέρας ἀμφὶ κινυρόμεναι προχέοντο,...

This is in turn drawn from the only bee-simile in Homer, at *Il.* 2.87-90:

---

[124] H. Dahlmann, "Der Bienenstaat in Vergils *Georgica*", *Abh. Akad. Mainz. Geistesw. Kl.* 547-562, stresses the political importance of the bees in both works, but neglects the crucial question of *amor*. E. W. Leach, "*Sedes Apibus* from the *Georgics* to the *Aeneid*", *Vergilius* 23 (1977), 2-20, discusses bees in the two poems and sees historical events preventing man from ever attaining the harmony of the bee-kingdom.

ἠΰτε ἔθνεα εἶσι μελισσάων ἀδινάων,
πέτρης ἐκ γλαφυρῆς αἰεὶ νέον ἐρχομενάων·
βοτρυδὸν δὲ πέτονται ἐπ' ἄνθεσιν εἰαρινοῖσιν·
αἱ μέν τ' ἔνθα ἅλις πεποτήαται, αἱ δέ τε ἔνθα·

Homer simply compares numbers and movement; his bees are a
homeless swarm. Apollonius contrasts the sweet setting of the simile
with the anxiety of the women in comparing their frenzied movement and murmuring. The simile in *Aeneid* 6 has a different purpose.
Virgil's first bee-simile had involved men at work; this one compares
idle souls. The Carthaginians were feverish, the souls are quiet and
slow. The former do their everyday tasks, the latter prepare for a
single, extraordinary event. This alone would be sufficient to show
that the bees are not simply a political symbol for Virgil, but rather
a higher symbol of happy concord among fellows.

The bees in Book 6 are explicit symbols of this reincarnated
harmony,[125] as if Virgil were making the terms of the simile perfectly clear. Porphyry, in his *Cave of the Nymphs* (18), explains the
bees of *Od.* 13.106 as allegorical souls returning to re-birth. The
souls at birth are not bees in fact, but are *like* bees as the Tyrians
were like bees, as the Golden Bough is like the mistletoe of the
Labyrinth. The bees, mentioned as immortal in *Geo.* 4.206-208,
partake of ethereal draughts (219-227) as does the shade, the only
part of man that remains after the purgation of the body. The
purified soul is therefore the soul free from the trammels of passionate love, which does not reproduce itself and has been made
famous by selfless sacrifice (6.664), just like the bees of *Geo.*
4.197-209.

This idea is picked up following the interview between Dido
and Aeneas when the souls lost in the Trojan War stand clustered
around him much as the bees clustered around their king: *Circumstant animae dextra laevaque frequentes.* (6.486) [126] Like the souls,
like the bees, Aeneas will learn the mysteries of the world and will
return to the realm of the living. But unlike these souls, he will
take with him and execute, as king, a specific prophecy of the
future. The simile assumes that along with the knowledge, he also
carries with him the harmony of the bee-community. The vision

---

[125] V. Pöschl, *The Art of Virgil: Image and Symbol in the Aeneid*, tr.
G. Seligson, Ann Arbor, 1962, 71-72.
[126] M. de G. Verrall, "Two Instances of Symbolism in the Sixth *Aeneid*",
*CR* 24 (1910), 43-46.

of Rome's future [127] and the bee-like quality of his soul equip
Aeneas for his mission and, once out of Hades, he never wavers in
his determination. It is as if the struggles through which he has
come are suddenly vindicated by this vision of death and resurrection, just as Aristaeus' disastrous loss of his entire hive can be
resolved by the knowledge of *bugonia*.

The bees of Book 7 are also closely associated with Aeneas as
harbingers of his (and the Aeneadae's) arrival in Latium:

> Laurus erat tecti medio in penetralibus altis
> sacra comam multosque metu servata per annos,
> quam pater inventam, primas cum conderet arces,
> ipse ferebatur Phoebo sacrasse Latinus
> Laurentisque ab ea nomen posuisse colonis.
> Huius apes summum densae (mirabile dictu)
> stridore ingenti liquidum trans aethera vectae
> obsedere apicem, et pedibus per mutua nexis
> examen subitum ramo frondente pependit.
>
> *(Aen.* 7.59-67)

The bees fly in a swarm, like the souls in Hades, not like the hive-
bees in Book 1, and light in the sacred laurel tree at the center of
Latinus' palace.[128] The association of the Trojans with a wandering
swarm, hinted at in the first simile, implied in the second, here
takes on the aspect of a concrete symbol. It is a prophecy that
Aeneas and his band will capture the citadel of Latinus.

More importantly, beyond the omen itself, is the interpretation
of the *vates*:

> Continuo vates: 'Externum cernimus' inquit
> 'adventare virum et partis petere agmen easdem
> partibus ex isdem et summa dominarier arce.'
>
> *(Aen.* 7.68-70)

Grant quotes the translation of C. Day Lewis: [129]

> I see a stranger coming.
> Men are coming from where the bees came—coming to settle
> Where the bees have settled, this fortress their seat of empire.

---

[127] See *Geo.* 4.216, *circumstant fremitu denso stipantque frequentes.*

[128] See *Geo.* 4.113. The Aeneadae began their journey at a laurel tree
outside Troy (2.715). Such a tree was also at Priam's palace (2.513).

[129] Grant, 391.

Aeneas has come from a bee-community to found another bee-community of his own. Yet he and his men are still the threatening *agmen* they had been in the ant-simile. We see then that the omen of the bee,[130] followed by a reminiscence of the ant-simile and association with Troy, inverts the terms of the earlier similes. Having witnessed the ruin of Troy and having ruined the ideal community of Carthage, Aeneas will now begin to forge a new one.

The bees of Book 12 are different.

> Saepe etiam effossis, si vera est fama, latebris
> sub terra fovere larem penitusque repertae
> pumicibusque cavis exessaeque arboris antro.
>
> *(Geo.* 4.42-44)

> Si quando sedem augustam servataque mella
> thensauris relines, prius haustu sparsus aquarum
> ora fove fumosque manu praetende sequacis...
> Illis ira modum supra est, laesaeque venenum
> morsibus inspirant et spicula caeca relinquont
> adfixae venis animasque in volnere ponunt.
>
> *(Geo.* 4.228-230, 236-238)

> inclusas ut cum latebroso in pumice pastor
> vestigavit apes fumoque implevit amaro;
> illae intus trepidae rerum per cerea castra
> discurrunt magnisque acuunt stridoribus iras;
> volvitur ater odor tectis, tum murmure caeco
> intus saxa sonant, vacuas it fumus ad auras.
>
> *(Aen.* 12.587-592)

The first *Georgics* passage describes the bees that live in rocks. These bees lurk (*latebris* and *latebroso*); the *Georgics* bees are poisonous (*venenum*) and fix their sting in the vein (*venis*) by which they leave their souls in the wound. The latter *Georgics* passage describes smoking the bees out of their hive. The hive is *augusta* ("stately"), while the bees in the simile live in coverts. The smoke in the *Georgics* is *sequax* ("searching", i.e. thoroughly cleaning) while the smoke in the *Aeneid* is *amarus*, "bitter," with an *odor ater* in order to drive them out of the rocks for good, and possibly to make the bees, in their anger, kill themselves by stinging their attackers.

---

[130] Anchises' prophecy of Rome's future greatness, especially the Catalogue of Heroes (777-853), involves the ideal of devotion and self-sacrifice on the one hand and the glory of the leaders on the other, qualities of the bees that Virgil has stressed.

The simile is paralleled in Apollonius *Arg.* 2.130-136, where the Argonauts rout the Bebrycians: [131]

ὡς δὲ μελισσάων σμῆνος μέγα μηλοβοτῆρες
ἠὲ μελισσοκόμοι πέτρῃ ἔνι καπνιόωσιν,
αἱ δ' ἤτοι τείως μὲν ἀολλέες ᾧ ἐνὶ σίμβλῳ
βομβηδὸν κλονέονται, ἐπιπρὸ δὲ λιγνυόεντι
καπνῷ τυφόμεναι πέτρης ἑκὰς ἀίσσουσιν·
ὣς οἵγ' οὐκέτι δὴν μένον ἔμπεδον, ἀλλ' ἐκέδασθεν
εἴσω Βεβρυκίης, Ἀμύκου μόρον ἀγγελέοντες·

Virgil has taken the comparison of the description of the disarray of the Bebrycians preceding their flight along with the mention of the shepherd and the bees holed up in a rock (πέτρῃ... ολέες ᾧ ἐνὶ σίμβλῳ = *inclusas... latebroso*) from this simile. But the bees in Apollonius flee their home, while Virgil's bees are trapped in theirs. The ideal community is destroyed amid panic, furious buzzing and the black stench of smoke.

The confusion of Turnus' men, likened to a swarm of bees, is altered slightly from *Geo.* 4.228-233. By now the prophecy of Book 7 has come true. The assault on the hive (bee-simile in *Aen.* 1) by a swarm (ant-simile in *Aen.* 4) is echoed as Aeneas, assured of power, roots out the last threatening swarm. The reign of Latinus had been one of peace, a veritable "golden age," comparable to the peaceful existence of the bees before the strife in *Geo.* 4.8-67. The victor in the conflict over Latium will be selected to rule as is the strong king in *Geo.* 4.88-102.

---

[131] Most bee-portents of this kind are negative as were the bees that gathered on Pompey's standard at Philippi and Scipio's at the Ticinus (Livy 21.46.2). But L. Herrmann, "Le quatrième livre des *Géorgiques* et les abeilles d'Actium", *REA* 33 (1931), 219-224, says that the importance of the bees in the *Georgics* derives from the reports of bees seen nesting in the prows and helmets washed ashore at Actium. He cites omens of bees in 218, 214, 208, 118, 104, and 92 B.C., as well as the bees that entered the camps of Cassius and Pompey before their respective defeats. Caesarians were victorious in both cases. As Herrmann puts it, the bees symbolize impending defeat. In the two examples closest in time to the composition of Virgil's poems, they presaged victory for the forces of Augustus as they presage victory for the forces of Aeneas in the *Aeneid*. The bees in the *Georgics* are neither ominous nor sinister but rather more like those living in the helmets at Actium in the poem of Philip of Thessalonica which first describes the bees in the prows and then concludes, Καίσαρος εὐνομίης χρηστὴ χάρις· ὅπλα γὰρ ἐχθρῶν/χαρποὺς εἰρήνης ἀντεδίδαξε τρέφειν. (*P.A.* 6.236). The bees as symbols of happy leadership are like those to which the Carthaginians are compared in *Aeneid* 1 and the bees that nest in Latinus' laurel in Book 7.

Finally, the simile reverses the terms of the fall of Troy, where the Trojans, trapped in the city amid the noise, confusion, and smoke are scattered or killed.[132] Aeneas is the agent, rather than the victim of such destruction in Book 12.

The symbolic (certainly not allegorical) use of the bees to which Virgil alludes while planning the *Aeneid* (*Geo.* 4.116-117 and, indirectly, 3-7) has been set at crucial points of his text and is present even at the core of his hero's "epiphany", Book 6. The bees, it may be argued, are Virgil's most original conception in either of his poems.[133] The superficial significance is clear, despite the admittedly mock-heroic treatment in *Georgics* 4 (the battles in particular): they are small, tough, efficient creatures, just like Roman citizens, whose lifestyle can be regulated by man as man's life can be regulated by the gods;[134] who, though small individually, are great and powerful collectively, and whose personal achievements are subservient to the society they serve, just as Aeneas' sufferings are important as they aid the founding of his nation.

Moreover, the bees are distinct metaphors related to the crucial themes of love and death in both poems. In the *Georgics*, their asexuality and the immortality of the hive had contrasted with the ruinous *amor* and death by plague of the beasts. Structurally, the description prepared for the union of the themes of love and death in man in the great Aristaeus episode. And stylistically, the mock-epic tone had prepared the reader for the fully epic tone of the Aristaeus tale while providing a source of battle-descriptions for the *Aeneid*. The various aspects of the bee-community find their way into many parts of the *Aeneid*, yet each major simile stresses a different characteristic (industry, harmony, portentousness, feroc-

---

[132] The only bee-simile in Homer is at *Il.* 2.87-93 where the Greeks assemble for a council as bees thronging from a rock. This simile does not appear to have influenced Virgil.

[133] On the symbolism of the hive as city, see R. W. Cruttwell, *Virgil's Mind at Work*, New York, 1969, 113-126 and, 126: "Aeneas... is mentally visualized by Virgil as shouldering the burden of that Trojan-Roman destiny whose Mediterranean symbol is a beehive-hut..." W. R. Johnson, in *Darkness Visible: A Study of Vergil's Aeneid*, Berkeley, 1976, views the similes lucidly, yet inexplicably finds the bee-simile of Book 12 reflects "a nightmare of civil war". (93) The emphasis is surely on the men routing the bees not simply on the panic within the hive.

[134] Like the motifs of the snake, oak, and storm, their major effect is in the first six books of the *Aeneid*, although the bees are more significant than these in Books 7 and 12.

ity), and is seen in other similes, especially that of the ant. These tiny creatures manifest the grandest themes, appearing like a chorus to certify the major events of the poem. Integrated subtly with patterns of narrative and simile, they hold a mirror to mankind and show him his world in little. *In tenui labor; at tenuis non gloria.*

## C. STORMS

Although it yields less material to the *Aeneid* than the rest of the *Georgics*,[135] Book I contains a memorable storm description which is recalled frequently throughout the epic. Modeled on the *Works and Days* of Hesiod, the book may be divided into three parts, the first devoted to knowledge of the soil and the value of hard work (43-203) and the second and third to the observation of the heavens in the "Farmer's Calendar" (204-350) and "Weather Signs" (351-423) sections.[136] Throughout each part, the moral sententiousness of Hesiod is blended with a number of themes, the humanization of the land and man's war-like struggle with it,[137] Italy and Foreign Lands,[138] and, departing from Hesiod (and Lucretius), the right rule of Jupiter, by whose planned design man must work, once the Golden Age has been lost. These are some of the major themes, but there are others.[139] The crucial theme, however, is stated in the first line, *quo sidere terram vertere*: one must look to the heavens for guidance in farming.

The first section outlines the difficulties of the farmer's harsh life, ending with the famous simile depicting the furious struggle just to stay even:

> sic omnia fatis
> in peius ruere ac retro sublapsa referri,
> non aliter quam qui adverso vix flumine lembum
> remigiis subigit, si bracchia forte remisit,
> atque illum in praeceps prono rapit alveus amni.

> *(Geo.* 1.199-203)

---

[135] This may be due to its "Hesiodic" and less epic nature or to the fact that it was completed well before the other three. See J. Bayet, "Les premiers 'Géorgiques' de Virgile", *RPh* 56 (1930), 128-150, 227-247.

[136] Otis (149) and Wilkinson (81-84) differ only slightly in their division of the book, and that in the last section.

[137] See Otis, 156 for examples of humanization here and for military metaphors, "Both men and the land are represented as engaged in a terrible struggle, man coming to the relief of a tormented earth whose fertility is constantly under attack". (155-156)

[138] See Wilkinson, 67.

[139] For mention of these themes see Wilkinson, 76-82.

But if Jupiter has ordained that life should be a toil for man, he has also given man the aid of the stars and the heavens, described in the "Farmer's Calendar." [140] Near the close of this section, Virgil illustrates the consequences of failure to observe the heavens with an epic storm whose focus, the stupefaction of the detached observer through whose eyes the storm is seen, is found in Homer, *Il.* 4.452-456: [141]

> ὡς δ᾽ ὅτε χείμαρροι ποταμοὶ κατ᾽ ὄρεσφι ῥέοντες
> ἐς μισγάγκειαν συμβάλλετον ὄβριμον ὕδωρ
> κρουνῶν ἐκ μεγάλων κοίλης ἔντοσθε χαράδρης,
> τῶν δέ τε τηλόσε δοῦπον ἐν οὔρεσιν ἔκλυε ποιμήν·
> ὡς τῶν μισγομένων γένετο ἰαχή τε πόνος τε.

Elements of this simile and other storm passages [142] are found in the storm in the *Georgics*:

> Saepe ego, cum flavis messorem induceret arvis
> agricola et fragili iam stringeret hordea culmo,
> omnia ventorum concurrere proelia vidi,
> quae gravidam late segetem ab radicibus imis
> 320 sublimem expulsam eruerent: ita turbine nigro
> ferret hiemps culmumque levem stipulasque volantes.
> Saepe etiam immensum caelo venit agmen aquarum,
> et foedam glomerant tempestatem imbribus atris
> collectae ex alto nubes; ruit arduus aether
> et pluvia ingenti sata laeta boumque labores
> diluit; implentur fossae et cava flumina crescunt
> cum sonitu fervetque fretis spirantibus aequor.
> Ipse pater media nimborum in nocte corusca
> fulmina molitur dextra; quo maxuma motu
> 330 terra tremit; fugere ferae, et mortalia corda
> per gentis humilis stravit pavor; ille flagranti
> aut Atho aut Rhodopen aut alta Ceraunia telo
> deicit; ingeminant Austri et densissimus imber;
> nunc nemora ingenti vento, nunc litora plangunt.

*(Geo.* 1.316-334)

Here, all the elements of nature are arrayed against man in a tremendous crescendo (wind, whirlwind, showers, flood). Then,

---

[140] This section corresponds to the "Days" section of Hesiod's poem. There is no strict Hesiodic counterpart for the "Weather-Signs" section of *Geo.* 1.

[141] See also *Il.* 4.275-282, the fire in *Il.* 2.455-458, and the work of the young men in *Il.* 5.87-88.

[142] Principally *Geo.* 3.97-100, *Aen.* 2.304-308, 12.451-455. For other parallels, see chart on p. 84.

dramatically at 328, Jupiter himself intervenes. This is not simply a misfortune for the farmer, but a vengeful (almost Old Testament-style) punishment for the farmer's neglect of the heavens. Apart from minor changes, Virgil's crucial addition to Homer is the embodiment of divine anger in the storm. As such, it ends its passage with a climactic *Schlussfigur*.

The third section of the book (351-514), which begins *Atque haec ut certis possemus discere signis... ipse pater statuit* (351-353), unites the farmer's struggle against nature to the decline from the Golden Age. With divine help, man can learn for himself the workings of the universe and strive towards a positive goal, not vainly toil to keep even in an ever-worsening situation. This harmony was *given* to man in the Golden Age, but Jupiter realized that it would ennoble man to *achieve* it by the *labor* both of his back and brain.

In short, the violence of nature represents in the *Georgics* and, as we shall see, in the *Aeneid*, both a divine threat to that civilizing impulse and a challenge to man to overcome it.

The farmer's life is linked to the contemporary Roman's life when the natural phenomena actually prophesy an historical event which threatens civilization, the death of Caesar. In this case, a natural event becomes an historical event (the portents recorded by the historians [143]): the meteorological reaction to Caesar's death heralds the coming civil strife. Like the storm in the second section, the end is not described, only the rising ferocity, after which there is a prayer for a savior (498-501), concluding the book on a pessimistic note as the simile at 202-203 and the rising tempest had ended other sections of the book.

The concept of the storm changes from a force which acts against man in the first section to one *with* which man can work, foretelling natural destruction by prognostics, until finally the storm entails moral or political destruction. It is this final symbolic use of elemental violence, coupled with the theme of man's effort to understand and respond to a divine will that defines the use of the storm similes and descriptions in the *Aeneid*.

---

[143] For the portents and their citations by Dio, Plutarch, Pliny, and Appian, see D. L. Drew, "The Structure of Vergil's *Georgics*", *AJP* 50 (1929), 246-248. It must be remembered, however, that these writers may be echoing Virgil's description, which in any case has many conventional aspects. See R. O. A. M. Lyne, " 'Scilicet et tempus veniet...' Virgil, *Geo.* 1.463-514", *Quality and Pleasure in Latin Poetry* ed. by T. Woodman and D. West, Cambridge, 1974, 51.

As the following table shows, nearly every line of the storm description is used in similes about the ferocity of men and gods in the *Aeneid*. (Asterisk denotes non-simile)

| Geo. I | Aeneid | Simile |
|---|---|---|
| 318 | 10.356-357 | Soldiers like battling winds |
| 319 | 2.416-418 | Soldiers like torrent |
|  | 12.523-525 | Aeneas and Turnus like torrents |
| 320-321 | 2.416-418 | Greeks like whirlwind at Troy |
|  | 10.603-604 | Aeneas' destructiveness like whirlwind and torrent |
|  | 12.923 | Aeneas' spear like whirlwind |
| 322 | 12.450 (4.404) | Aeneas like storm-cloud |
| 323-324 | 5.317 | Runners like storm-cloud |
| 324 | *1.129 | *ruit arduus aether* |
| 325 | 2.306 | Battle (?) like fire |
| 327 | *7.24 | *vada fervida* |
|  | *10.291 | *vada spirant* |
| 328-329 | 5.319 | Nisus swifter than winds or lightning |
|  | 8.391-392 | Words like lightning (*corusco*) |
| 330-331 | 12.920 | Men frightened by spear as by lightning, hills resound with crash, *terra tremit.* |
| 331-333 | 12.701-702 | Aeneas big as mountains |
| 333-334 | 10.97-99 | Murmur of rising winds and Rumor |

Most of these repetitions are self-explanatory. The following discussion will concentrate on the use of storm phenomena in three similes: *Aen.* 2.304-318, 416-419, and 12.451-455.

Storms and related phenomena in *Aeneid* 1-6 are particularly associated with events motivated by *furor* and often serve as signs unperceived by the victim (Aeneas), but unmistakable to the reader. The *furor* is Juno's and twice the storms are motivated by agents (Aeolus and Anna). They imperil Aeneas each time, but more significant than the meteorological activity are his three very different reactions to them.

The importance of the storm-motif in the *Aeneid* is at once made clear by the fact that the poem begins with a storm (1.34-123), which is both a symbolic expression of the contention of the gods (Juno and Venus) and a mirror of the conflict within Aeneas. Also contrasted are, as Otis says, "*furor* and *pietas* with which the parallel contrast of fate (Jupiter) and counter-fate (Juno) is fully cor-related." [144] In Book 1, the jealous rage of Juno contrasts with the *pietas* of Venus in seeking her father's aid for the Trojans.

---

[144] Otis, 228.

Aeneas, however, shows both deep despair (in the "storm" section) and courage or *pietas* (in the "calm" section).[145] The storm off Carthage confirms to the reader (if not to Aeneas) that dangers lie ahead and that the gods have a hand in them. Aeneas yields not to *furor* but to despair (*Talia voce refert curisque ingentibus aeger/ spem vultu simulat, premit altum corde dolorem,* 208-209).

Much more can be said of the storm, but for our purposes here, we should only stress that the storm is an actual event (i.e. not a simile) which also initiates the terms of the storm-similes in Books 1-6: they are caused by the *furor* of Juno. "The storm is only a symbol of another storm to come but this later storm is not primarily physical but psychological and the calm itself is therefore deceptive.", says Otis.[146]

As the rural storm in the *Georgics* anticipates the civil storm at Rome, so the sea-storm heralds political strife at Carthage (the machinations of *Fama* and rejection of Iarbas). As the rage of Jupiter destroyed the incautious farmer's crops, so the rage of Juno at being ignored by mortals (1.37-75) causes the near-destruction of Aeneas' mission.

At *Aen.* 2.304-308, Aeneas sees the destruction of his native city as an *inscius pastor* watching the ruin of the farmer's land by fire and flood.

> in segetem veluti cum flamma furentibus Austris
> incidit aut rapidus montano flumine torrens
> sternit agros, sternit sata laeta bovumque labores
> praecipitisque trahit silvas; stupet inscius alto
> accipiens sonitum saxi de vertice pastor.

The difference from *Il.* 4.452-456 (quoted above) is clear. Virgil, like Homer, speaks of a raging force of soldiers.[147] But Homer simply uses the overhearing shepherd in the simile to stress the great din of battle and provide a peaceful contrast momentarily to the deathly business of the battle. The shepherd is not directly identified with any participant in the battle, unless with the reader who might recall a similar experience. Virgil clearly relates the shepherd to Aeneas, a lone figure threatened by the fearsome warriors, in order to stress the shepherd's (and therefore Aeneas')

---

[145] Ibid., 230.
[146] Ibid., 234.
[147] Greeks and Trojans in Homer, Greeks in Virgil.

ignorance of and unpreparedness for the storm. As such, the events
are vividly depicted through the mind of a character actually
involved in the narrative, using fire and flood symbolically to
depict the fear and anxiety in his own mind. The simile therefore
serves not only to ornament and crystallize a significant moment
in the action, but also to explain the motivation of Aeneas' subsequent behavior. When he sees his city falling, his immediate
response is to fight Juno's *furor* with his own (315, 355), but he
fails. The same winds of the sea-storm return at *Aen.* 2.416-419
(again compared to Greek soldiers), but the source is different,
*Il.* 14.396-401.[148]

Between fleeing the storm-like Greeks and suffering the actual
storm at sea, Aeneas had endured the storm off Crete before the
Harpies attacked (3.192-208) and was similarly passive and perplexed. Immediately afterwards, the long prophecy of Helenus
warns him of the storm:

> Iunoni cane vota libens dominamque potentem
> supplicibus supera donis; sic denique victor
> Trinacria finis Italos mittere relicta.
>
> (3.438-440)

The storms of the *Georgics* and *Aeneid* I are recalled in Book 4:

> incipiunt...resonantia longe/litora misceri
>
> (*Geo.* 1.357-359)
>
> Interea magno misceri murmure pontum
>
> (*Aen.* 1.124)
>
> Interea magno misceri murmure caelum/incipit
>
> (*Aen.* 4.160-161)

Again the storm is sent by Juno, but this time with the foolish
aid of Venus. Like the storm in *Aeneid* I, it is both an actual event
(it forces the union of Dido and Aeneas, as the storm at sea had
forced their meeting) and a proleptic one, a prophecy of the psycho-

---

[148] There are two other storm-similes in *Aeneid* 2 (494-499, Greeks break
into Priam's sanctum like a river flooding its banks, and 516, Hecuba and
her daughters quail like doves in a storm). Putnam, 6-8, notes that the
Trojan horse is compared to a mountain (2.15), like the mountain of Aeolus
whence the storm in *Aeneid* I came. Violence is also seen in *Geo.* 1.482-483
and *Aen.* 2.498-499. See L. Vischi, "Similitudini virgiliane", *C & N* 5 (1909),
245-246 for a discussion of this.

logical storm to come.[149] The *furor* belongs to both Juno and Dido and, like the previous storm, the ending of the symbolic storm is the beginning of the human, psychological one.

Finally, when Aeneas is buffeted like an oak tree (again by the will of Juno), he remains firm in his resolution, determined to follow the law of Fate, to leave Carthage and Dido. He becomes the instrument of his destiny, and his simple endurance of the storm is a more positive and successful act than any kind of furious retaliation.[150]

How then does this motif relate to the *Georgics*? Of primary importance is the humanization. Drawing on Homer, Virgil stresses the human consequences of the storms by having them twice viewed by ignorant observers. Therefore, it is not the power or cruelty or noise of the storm that is important, but rather the *effect* of the storm on its observer and/or victim.

Second, the storms are put at climactic points of the narrative, at the very beginning of the poem, at the fall of Troy, the rendezvous of Aeneas and Dido, and their final parting. The storm passage had occupied an equally significant position in *Georgics* 1. The ignorant victim of nature's fury in that book becomes in *Aeneid* 1-4 a victim of human and divine disturbance. The storm in the *Georgics* had been a thunderstorm ruining the plantation of the unwary farmer. By the end of the book, odd weather presages the danger to Rome itself. In the same way, Aeneas progresses from an ignorant victim of the heavenly will to its agent and symbol. As man had been first a victim of the storm (the farmer in *Geo.* 1.316-334), but became a cause of the storm (political man in *Geo.* 1.461-497), so also with Aeneas. In both poems nature and historical disasters are expressed as results of the divine will. In both, man must learn to know the divine will by work and observation. When the farmer learns the order of the heavens, as when Aeneas finally accepts his destiny, he is a master; until that time he is a victim.[151] Whether a particular storm is good or evil is less important than

---

[149] Again, this involves a conflict in Aeneas' mind, but the real conflict is between Aeneas and Dido.

[150] Similarly, Palinurus at 5.1-34 sees the divine will in the storm. He is taken by Neptune in 779-781 as a payment for calming the sea, a sign that the Trojans no longer need a navigator.

[151] Likewise, the Trojans may be seen to change from passive victims of the storm in 9.25-26, 30-32, and 433-437 to agents in 9.668-671 and 11.624-635.

the fact that it is part of Jupiter's (and therefore Fate's) system of governance. It is the duty of man to learn both the signs and the source of the storms. As such, Virgil stresses his philosophy of divine involvement in human affairs, in opposition to the view of his chief Latin model, Lucretius, that the gods (even if they exist), play no role in human affairs: *pater ipse colendi/haut facilem esse viam voluit.* (*Geo.* 1.121)

In Books 7-9, the storms are much more like their conventional Homeric counterparts, depicting men in battle without necessarily cohering into a specific pattern. They are associated with *furor*, to be sure, but they do not involve Aeneas, only the armies contending in his absence.[152] They are still pictured as destructive but, with the peculiar exception of the accidental shower that breaks the poppy in the simile of Euryalus' death (9.436-437), they do not apply to individuals. No one is as ignorant or unaware of the storm as was Aeneas, although the storms are provoked by definite causes which the victims should have recognized. In short, these storms reflect nothing more than skirmishes before the battle royal. With the hero's return from Pallanteum, the war is gradually reduced to a struggle between Aeneas and Turnus, culminating in the final *monomachia* in Book 12, done in images of the violence of nature.

The final episodes of the war itself, in Books 10-12 are both predicted and waged in terms of storms.

The quantitative bulk of the storm similes occurs in Book 10, preparing for the final battle. At 10.96-99, Juno concludes her reply to Venus, and the gods in council murmur like the wind in the trees which foretells a coming storm to sailors. This is paralleled by the Latins' reaction to Venulus' account of Diomede's encouragement of peace with the Trojans. The Latins murmur like waters of a flood pent up behind rocks in 11.296-299. Both similes warn of the coming strife, one at the divine level, one at the human.

When Aeneas finally returns, two similes compare his approach to storm-signs seen in the *Georgics*. When the Trojans see him,

---

[152] 7.523-530, Trojan and Latin youths are like the sea whipped by winds; 585-590, Latinus is like a rock beaten by waves (compare the simile of Aeneas as a tree nestled in crags in Book 4 and Dido as rock in Book 6), 718-721, the Latin troops are like a storm at sea, 9.25-26, 30-32, the armies of the Latins and the shields of the Latins are like rainstorms in winter (cf. *Aen.* 5.458-460), and the storm caused by Jupiter at 9.670-671.

they release their spears with a shout, as the cranes fly with shrieks before a storm (262-266). This Trojan reaction is balanced by Turnus' reaction. He sees the boss of Aeneas' shield as a baneful comet glowing in the night or like Sirius, the bringer of plague and pestilence.[153]

> Taygete simul os terris ostendit honestum
> Pleas et Oceani spretos pede reppulit amnis,
> aut eadem sidus fugiens ubi Piscis aquosi
> tristior hibernas caelo descendit in undas.
>
> (Geo. 4.232-235)

> Iam rapidus torrens sitientis Sirius Indos
> ardebat caelo et medium sol igneus orbem
> hausserat...
>
> (Geo. 4.425-427)

> non secus ac liquida si quando nocte cometae
> sanguinei lugubre rubent, aut Sirius ardor
> ille sitim morbosque ferens mortalibus aegris
> nascitur et laevo contristat lumine caelum.
>
> (Aen. 10.272-275)

Virgil adds to these similes the prospect of approaching calamity. While drawn from *Il.* 5.5, the comet in the *Aeneid* is clearly like the comet in *Geo.* 1.488 that appears after Caesar's death.[154]

These similes then signify on the human level what the first simile signified on the divine level: the imminence of conflict. At 10.356-361, the battle itself is described as a contention of winds, much as is the battle at Troy.

The first comparison of a violent natural force to a single person occurs in the description of Pallas in battle at 10.405-411. He is like a shepherd kindling fire here and there in the woods when the winds he has longed for have arisen (*optato ventis aestate coortis*). This may recall the shepherd of *Aen.* 2.304-308 who was passive

---

[153] Aeneas' armor had been described in 8.619-623 as glowing red as the sky when the sunlight is refracted through the clouds. The simile is probably from *Il.* 11.64-66, a similar description of Hector with his shield. Virgil adds the comparison of Priam to the dog-star (from *Il.* 22.26-29) but elaborates the destruction in terms from the *Georgics*. There is also a reminiscence of the simile used to describe Jason at *Arg.* 3.957-958, without mention of plague and drought.

[154] R. J. Getty, "Some Astronomical Cruces in the *Georgics*" *TAPA* 79 (1948), 40-43, says both clauses refer to the time following the summer solstice, while Richter (364) says that Sirius (literally, "The Scorcher") stands for the sun and is a variation on the first clause.

and perplexed, while here, Pallas is active and determined. But
he is unwittingly causing his own destruction, for his murderous
careering about the field forces a battle between him and Turnus
(*soli mihi Pallas/debetur* says Turnus in 442-443) in which he is
easily and cruelly slain (454-456). He has in effect caused his own
destruction even though he is successful for a while. Nevertheless,
the description of his momentary joy at enflaming his forces certainly recalls its earlier models in the *Aeneid* and *Georgics*:

> ille sedens victor flammas despectat ovantis
>
> (*Aen.* 10.409)

After Pallas is killed, the final shift of terms occurs when Aeneas,
formerly the passive, confused victim of the storms of others'
wrath, becomes the active, determined, wrathful storm himself.[155]
In 10.602-604, he clears a path from the ships to the camp like a
raging flood or a black whirlwind. He now embodies the destruction
his armor had prophesied. As he goes to meet Mezentius in 10.693-
701, he is compared to a rain-storm attacking a rock. This simile
recalls both the comparison of Latinus to a sea-lashed cliff in *Aen.*
7.586-590 (he can endure the threats of war but cannot prevent
war itself) and the oak tree in Book 4 which prevails over the winds
that buffet it.

After Aeneas wounds Mezentius, the Latins redouble their
attack on him and he retreats to a cave as one taking shelter from
a storm (*nubem belli*) (10.801-810). Aeneas has *furor* (*furit Aeneas*),
but, like the ploughman in the *Georgics* (1.259-267) who hones his
blade indoors, Aeneas wisely prepares for battle by playing on
Lausus' vulnerability to *furor*, rather than being victimized by
his own. At 11.624-635, the beleaguered Latins fleeing and re-
taliating are compared to a giant wave breaking and receding.

In 12.450, the words *rapit agmen aperto* recall *Geo.* 1.322 and
*Aen.* 4.404, the column of wind and the column of ants. Virgil
then says:

> Qualis ubi ad terras abrupto sidere nimbus
> it mare per medium (miseris, heu, praescia longe
> horrescunt corda agricolis: dabit ille ruinas
> arboribus stragemque satis, ruet omnia late),
> ante volant sonitumque ferunt ad litora venti:
>
> (*Aen.* 12.451-455)

---

[155] See Hornsby, 38-40, 124-125.

Here the parallels are clear: the *miseri agricolae* did not foresee the storm and can only watch, like the farmer in *Geo.* 1.[156]

Finally, in Book 12, Aeneas himself becomes the storm. The simile at *Aen.* 12.451-455, as I have already mentioned, is a complement to the simile in Book 2 where Aeneas is the *inscius pastor*. Here he is the harbinger of storms and the Rutulians are frightened farmers (*horrescunt corda agricolis*). The crucial parallel, however, is with the farmer caught unawares by the storm in *Geo.* 1.316-334.[157] In the simile in Book 12, the farmers are aware (*praescia*), but the results are the same; the crops are ruined, trees are destroyed, and general havoc ensues. The distinction is that these farmers see the cloud as a storm-sign as the farmer in the *Georgics* did not. The point made here is that now both sides are aware of the fated outcome of the war: it is as inevitable as the predicted storm.

At *Aen.* 12.521-528, Aeneas and Turnus in battle are both described as foaming rivers rushing down the sides of mountains causing destruction. This looks back to the same simile in Book 2 where Aeneas had been the victim of the Greeks who fell on Troy like an overflowing river. Again, he has become a storm of the kind that once attacked him.

Finally, at *Aen.* 12.923-925, Aeneas' spear which pierces Turnus is compared to a black whirlwind. Aeneas is now the agent of storms, one who, like Aeolus, unleashes his fury on others.

## CONCLUSIONS

In this chapter, we have seen 15 narrative passages in the *Georgics* provide objects of comparison for 33 similes in the *Aeneid* or roughly 20% of its total 160 similes. Subtracting the 38 brief similes, the proportion is closer to 30%. I have tried to demonstrate that the subject-matter of many of these similes is drawn from the traditional use of nature similes in epic. Virgil borrows such subject-matter to elevate the tone and universalize the context of the *Georgics*, but he adapts them in his own fashion, fitting the action of the Homeric similes into his narrative, putting a Homeric simile together with an Apollonian, comparing large

---

[156] For *abrupto sidere*, see *Aen.* 3.422, *Geo.* 3.259. Heaven is torn like a curtain and rain pours through the rift in the cloud. Cf. *Aen.* 9.671, Pliny, *N.H.* 2.131-134. The simile is from *Il.* 4.275-282.

[157] There is a curious *hantise verbale* in *satis...late* (12.454) and *sata laeta* in *Geo.* 1.335 and *Aen.* 2.306.

things to small, and so on. In short, his technique of elaborating a theme by means of an epic description or simile recalls a name not mentioned often in these pages, Lucretius. The relief by poetic digression of didactic exposition may be the most Lucretian element of Virgil's style in the *Georgics*. But this subject must await a fuller treatment.[158] The central point is that all of these characteristics are seen in Virgil long before he began using similes in the *Aeneid*.

The similes in the *Aeneid* that are drawn from narrative passages in the *Georgics* have many of the same structural functions as the similes in the *Georgics* discussed in the previous chapter. In addition, they reveal a very personal conception of nature. As others have pointed out, creatures and elements of nature are, if not humanized, at least fully sentient in the *Aeneid* and I hope to have shown that the principal source for this was the *Georgics*.

Large animals (and the oak tree) are compared to individuals in the *Aeneid*, each time exhibiting a single unique trait: the paternal patience of the tree, the skittish anxiety of the deer, the bold passion of the horse, or the stubborn pride of the bull. These animals are more than simple metaphors. Their behavior is motivated by the humanity that Virgil gives them: the tree actually weeps and groans, the bull feels shame and ambition, the horse is vain and arrogant and sexual. In addition, the tree and horse have been trained in the same terms as human children. These personalities, as I have tried to show, are all directly drawn from those established for their predecessors in the *Georgics*.

The smaller animals (except for the snake) occur in groups and tend to reflect elements of social behavior. These similes, linked into motifs, go further than Homer's by developing from comparisons of one action or motivation (e.g., the rage of a hungry lion compared to the rage of a battle-hungry warrior) into abstract expressions of good, evil, industry, fidelity, etc.

Such "abstractions" generally elaborate a motif in the *Georgics*. The ants which were merely hard-working pests in the *Georgics* become (in conjunction with the bees) symbols of villainous perfidy at Carthage. The birds, playful as soldiers on furlough, become pathetic symbols for victims of lost causes like Hecuba and Juturna.[159] The snake, a symbol of sudden violence in the earlier

---

[158] See B. Otis, (Ch. I, n. 8), 1-28.

[159] This treatment is presaged by the nightingale-Orpheus simile in the fourth *Georgic*.

poem, becomes the outstanding motif of *Aeneid* 2, developing from a concealed attacker to a symbol of patent violence (in its comparison to Pyrrhus). The bees that had stood for political man, patriotic and asexual, later stand for different characteristics at each appearance (industry, harmony, auspiciousness, ferocity), but each time signify the presence of Jupiter (Fate) in the events of the narrative. Finally, the storms, which in the *Georgics* had resulted from Jupiter's anger at man's ignorance or neglect of the heavens, become omens or manifestations of conflict and so certify the congruity of human and divine anger at crucial points of the poem. The *Aeneid* thus expands elements which were seminal in the *Georgics*.

There is an additional point of interest about the difference between some individuals and groups as they occur in the *Aeneid*. Virgil usually describes the individual animals in terms of their humanized behavior. The point about the descriptions and similes of the bulls, horses, deer and the individual birds is to impress upon the reader how like man these animals behave.[160] With some groups of animals, Virgil goes beyond this, emphasizing both the observation of these "human" traits by a character in the poem and their effect upon him. The serpent in *Aeneid* 2, as in the *Georgics*, is not only humanized, but is also seen by a man and frightens him. In the same way, the Trojans (ants) are seen by their victim Dido, as the Carthaginians (bees) were seen by Aeneas.[161] These images reflect the working of nature upon man and this, the very subject of the *Georgics*, shows a further, if more subtle, relationship between the two poems.

Of course, these symbols and descriptions do not carry equal weight in both poems. The tree, the birds, the snakes, and ants are relatively unimportant in the *Georgics* while the storm, bees, cattle and horses are intimately related to the structure and themes of both poems. In addition, most of the motifs we have studied in the *Aeneid* (snake, oak, ants, bees, storms) figure more prominently in the first six books.

One final conclusion to be drawn is that the similes of the larger animals display a humanized and emotional interpretation of the events of life, a personal, subjective version of objective activity.

---

[160] This is true of the description and simile of the oak tree, also.

[161] In the same way, the storm in *Aeneid* 2.304-308 is seen by Aeneas as if he were an *inscius pastor*.

It may not be a transcendental view of all nature as one, but this humanization at least reflects a cosmic sympathy for the creatures of nature upon whom irrational forces play. The smaller animals often represent some of these irrational forces (evil, anger, pity) more abstractly while the bees and storms more directly involve the will of Jupiter and the working of Fate.

I must add, having said this, that not all of the similes taken from the *Georgics* fit so carefully into the motifs described. *Aeneid* 5 in particular seems regularly to reverse the tone of the established motifs. The chariot-race at 5.144-147 and the arrows of 5.242-243 reverse their prior dramatic function. Another example is 5.267-283, in which the crippled barque of Sergestus, finishing the boat race after the awards have been given, is compared with the crippled snake in *Geo.* 3.422-424. Like the snake, the captain is embittered and frustrated in his defeat. But the simile occurs in a light passage: the spectators' reaction is laughter. There is no Homeric counterpart of this simile: it seems wholly suggested by the passage in the *Georgics*.[162] In both cases, we are meant to see the agony of the defeated, but the effects are vastly different from the malevolence of the snake in the rest of the poem.

There is one further point to be raised. I have stated that approximately one-third of the *Aeneid* similes owe some direct debt to the *Georgics*. What can we say of the two-thirds that do not? The numerical percentages may well be misleading, for clearly the major motifs of the *Aeneid* are those we have studied in this chapter. One-fourth of the remaining similes (43 of 160) compare something to human activity and 25 more are brief.

Yet there is clearly the same humanization of natural objects in these comparisons. The likening of Trojan children to dolphins frisking about in the water (*Aen.* 5.592-595) is of a kind with the playful birds of *Georgics* 2. The children have a *ludus*, the dolphins *ludunt*. The twin flower similes that depict the death of Euryalus at *Aen.* 9.435-437 show a humanization as delicate as that of the oak tree was harsh. The purple flower dies (*moriens*), the poppies have a weary neck (*lasso . . . collo*) and drop their head (*caput*). These similes show, in different degrees, the same structural importance and dramatic force that we have observed in similes drawn from the *Georgics*.[163]

---

[162] Lines 277-278 echo *Geo.* 3.416.
[163] On the irony of the dolphin simile, see Putnam, 86-87.

A minor motif can show the same traits. In *Aen.* 9.792-796, Turnus' advance into the Trojan camp has been checked. At the moment of his reversal he is compared to a lion beset by a crowd with raised spears. The lion is frightened (*territus*) but fierce (*acerbo*) and his *ira* and *virtus* prevent him from turning tail even though he cannot fight through the opposing crowd. Not only are the action and emotion (*ira*) of Turnus and the lion identical, but the motivation, the sense of human *virtus* is shared. The simile precedes his rout and embarrassment at the hands of the leaderless Trojans and intensifies his anger yet further.

This image is picked up at 10.454-456 where Virgil actually states that the resemblance to a lion, *meditans in proelia*, is an *imago Turni*. Here the mad beast (Turnus) and the easy victim (Pallas) are characterized before their confrontation. But the simile effectively shows that just as cattle are no match for the lion, and any contest between them could scarcely be considered a *proelium*, so Turnus is most craven in fighting the youth.

Finally, at the beginning of Book 12, Turnus becomes not only a lion in retreat, but a wounded one as well.

> Poenorum qualis in arvis
> saucius ille gravi venantum volnere pectus
> tum demum movet arma leo gaudetque comantis
> excutiens cervice toros fixumque latronis
> inpavidus frangit telum et fremit ore cruento:
> haud secus accenso gliscit violentia Turno.
>
> (*Aen.* 12.4-9)

Pöschl first compared this simile to its Homeric counterpart (*Il.* 20.164, Achilles fighting Aeneas is like a sleeping lion only roused to battle when wounded) to show how appropriate the wound is to the doomed Turnus (and *not* to Achilles).[164] Not only is there the subjective description (*movet arma... gaudet*, his attacker is a *latro*, a bandit) and the summary characterization of Turnus (*gliscit violentia*) but there are associations with two other motifs drawn from the *Georgics*: Dido, Aeneas' other antagonist, was a fatally wounded doe in Book 4 and in Book 12.101-102, the bulls rage in battle with a similar ferocity.[165] The simile, at the very beginning of this final book, summarizes the madness of Turnus which will lead to his death at the end.

---

[164] Pöschl, 109-111.
[165] See Otis, 372-373.

There are other lion similes in the *Aeneid* [166] and they bear some relationship to this motif. There are Homeric counterparts for the similes I have discussed [167] but no direct sources in the *Georgics*. We can, however, see that these lion similes humanize the beast beyond the Homeric limits, specifically identify the motivation of the comparand, and occupy important structural positions in their episodes. These characteristics are the essence of the narrative technique with which similes are employed in the *Georgics*, and are observable in the *Aeneid*, even in non-*Georgics* material.

---

[166] Turnus is compared to a lion at 9.792 and 10.454. He is compared to a tiger at 9.730. Other lion similes occur at 9.339 (Nisus), 551 (Helenor), 10.723 (Mezentius).

[167] For 9.792-796, see *Il.* 11.548ff., 17.109ff., 657ff. For 10.454-456, see *Il.* 5.161ff., 12.293.

# CHAPTER THREE

## CONCLUSIONS

It is possible that Virgil was adapting Homeric language to his personal style as early as eight years before he began work on the *Aeneid*. One may say that it was in part the application of this language, in conjunction with Virgil's unique view of nature, that transformed and elevated his didactic beyond the level of its predecessors. The Alexandrians had found it diverting to exhaust troves of carefully refined techniques and thoroughly researched lore in order to produce ingenious poetical descriptions of the cures for snake bites, the keeping of bees, or the movement of stars. Yet for them, the use of epic language and similes served only to reinforce the incongruously lofty treatment of the lowly subject. Virgil was able to employ many of the Alexandrian techniques, but it was essential that his style match his theme, that there be no hint of the tongue-in-cheek character of some of his Hellenistic models. He was, after all, not writing the *Georgics* for a limited audience either of farmers or of literary partisans; he was expressing a tenet of Augustan ideology that lay close to his heart and was meant to be communicated to the widest possible audience.

In making the message of his didactic poem intelligible to the Romans of his day, Virgil faced many problems that would recur in writing the *Aeneid*. The moral fract of Hesiod was as outworn as the mythology of Homer. The poetic value of these works was as outmoded by the public taste for the precious language and punctilious lore of the Neoterics as their ethical value was displaced by the cynicism generated over a century of political and social upheaval. In both poems, it was Virgil's amalgamation of old and new styles overlaid with his particular empathy for the *res naturae*, be they animal or vegetable, beast or human, that transformed the poems into unique creations.

The single point I would emphasize is that this process of transformation, which reached its height in the *Aeneid*, is observable throughout the *Georgics*, a fact overlooked or underplayed by many commentators and critics. The combination of styles is most clearly seen in the longer passages in which the actual structure of the poem is determined by the use of already distinctive similes and descriptions.

Nearly one-third of the similes in the *Aeneid* are drawn from the *Georgics* and most of these have parallels in prior epic. The similes in the *Georgics* are usually *Schlussfiguren*, clinching conclusions to climactic passages, often giving a human quality to some element of nature. Such similes are generally scarce in didactic and much more characteristic of an epic style like that of the *Aeneid*. These similes share many of the functions of the Lucretian "digression" in that they develop a motif into a dramatic statement that reflects a theme of the whole work. The debt to Lucretius, the first Roman to write of "jealous" (*invida*) nature and to describe the attraction and repulsion of atoms as "love" and "hate", is obvious.

This is by no means to say that Virgil could not have written the *Aeneid* exactly as he did without having written the *Georgics*. I do not wish to stress any derivativeness of the *Aeneid* to the expense of the originality of the *Georgics*. Virgil added, in selecting material from the handbooks of Varro and others for his didactic poem, ready-made natural descriptions contained in epic similes. These similes from earlier epic used as narrative in the *Georgics* not only elevated the language and tone of the poem, but compelled a comparison with human behavior of the behavior of animals and natural phenomena. One is so used to seeing angry men compared to raging storms or hungry lions that descriptions of such storms or lions make us naturally think of angry men. These epic reminiscences thus inform the entire thematic structure of the poem and, rather than acting as embellishments added to glorify the subject, assume an integral role in the depiction of its theme. This crucial feature of the style of the *Georgics* has gone largely unnoticed.

My final point is that these longer passages in the *Aeneid* that recall the *Georgics* appear most frequently in those books which we know were finished earliest. They seem not at all "props" to sustain the narrative flow during the initial stages of composition; some appear rather to be elements added during the latter stages of composition to include such extended motifs as the bees and ants in 1 and 4, the serpent in 2, and the trip to the underworld in 6. If these elements were not added late, we should expect more of them in the remaining books of the *Aeneid*.

I have limited this study to discussion of certain elements of the *Georgics* repeated by means of similes in the *Aeneid*. Exigencies of space prevent any thorough consideration of other kinds of repetitions, however brief or extensive they may be. Apart from those mentioned in the Introduction, some other kinds of repetition should be at least mentioned before I conclude.

Descriptions of animals in both poems show many of the traits seen in the similes. The goats and deer that ramble in the woods but come home at night in *Geo.* 3.316 and *Aen.* 7.491, the bullocks and heifers, bulls and ewes awaiting sacrifice in *Geo.* 4.540, 551, and *Aen.* 6.38, the golden-filletted bull before the altar in *Geo.* 1.217, *Aen.* 5.366, 9.627 are empathetically described in each poem. This empathy is transferred to men when an animal description is applied to men without the aid of a simile (as in *Geo.* 4.83 and *Aen.* 5.805 where the description of the bee, as small in stature but a warrior nonetheless, is applied to Tydeus). In *Geo.* 1.403, the little owl prays for rain in vain (*seros cantus*) while in *Aen.* 12.861-866, the Fury Megaera is transformed into something like an owl (*alitis parvae*) which sings its late song (*serum canit*). In *Geo.* 3.523, the word *inertia* is used to describe the dumb animals awaiting their doom in the plague while the same word is used of the Trojans in *Aen.* 2.364 who are like dumb animals awaiting their fate. But such a listing of parallel descriptions could go on indefinitely.

Much of this book has dealt with the transference of elements from didactic parts of the *Georgics* to the *Aeneid*. I should like finally to examine an epic passage used in both poems so that I might review my procedures and conclusions in general and, more specifically, show how Virgil adapts non-simile epic material from the one poem for use in the other.

Perhaps the best example is the loss of Eurydice (*Geo.* 4.481-527) and the loss of Creusa (*Aen.* 2.559-795). We know that in earlier versions of the myth, Aeneas' wife was named Eurydica and, perhaps feeling that the name could not be dissociated from the Orpheus legend, Virgil accepted the account (as did Livy and others of his time) that her name was Creusa.[1] Yet, as several critics have pointed out, it seems clear that the other Eurydice, likewise a lost wife, was in the poet's mind as he described Aeneas' last moments at Troy.[2] I shall give a brief outline of the verbal and structural parallels.

---

[1] Pausanias 10.26.1 and Ennius *An.* 37 call her Eurydica while Livy 1.3.2. and others call her Creusa. See Austin, II, 287-289.

[2] Most major works on Virgil comment on the similarity of the scenes. The three most useful discussions are: J. Heurgon, "Un exemple peu connu de la *retractatio* virgilienne" *REL* 9 (1931), 258-268, an analysis of the

Orpheus and Aeneas both attempt their exits with their wives (*coniuge-Geo*. 4.504, *dulcis coniunx-Aen*. 2.777) behind them (*pone sequens-*487, *pone subit coniunx-*725). As they near the end (*superas veniebat ad auras-*486, *Iamque propinquabam portis-*730), having escaped all danger (*Iamque... casus evaserat omnis-*485, *Iamque... omnemque videbar/evasisse viam-*730-731), each is distracted (Orpheus by a *dementia*, Aeneas by a *male numen amicum*), Orpheus and Creusa halt (*restitit-*490, *substitit-*739), the husbands look back (*respexit-*491, *respexi-*741) and are rebuked for their madness (*Quis tantus furor?-*495, *Quid tantum insano iuvat indulgere dolori..-*776), losing their loves, never to be restored again (*neque... praeterea vidit-*500-502, *nec post oculis est reddita nostra-*740). After the loss, both men fill up the region around them with laments (Orpheus as nightingale *maestis late loca questibus implet-*515, Aeneas says *implevi clamore vias maestusque...-*769)³ and vainly clutch at their women (*prensantem nequiquam-*501, *Ter conatus ibi collo dare bracchia circum-*792), who disappear like smoke or air (*ceu fumus in auras... tenuis-*499-500, *tenuisque recessit in auras... par levibus ventis-*791-794), saying, "*Iamque vale*" (497, 789).⁴

---

sources for the Eurydice tale and a comparison of the Eurydice and Creusa Episodes; Putnam, (Ch. II, n. 38), 41-48, a treatment of the episodes along with the account of Aeneas' descent to the Underworld to show that Orpheus' poetry and Aeneas' destiny are their chief weapons in their struggles; and C. P. Segal (Ch. I, n. 12), who treats ten instances of vanishing souls throughout the *Aeneid* and shows how each compares with the loss of Eurydice in terms of the degree of pathos or objectivity required. All three cite verbal parallels between the two episodes.

³ The cries of Aeneas at 2.768-770 resemble those of Orpheus' disembodied head at *Geo*. 4.523-527.

⁴ To these verbal and structural parallels may be added other characteristics common to both poems such as the tendency to end books with dramatic episodes (the storm in *Geo*. 1, the "Country Life" in 2, the plague in 3, the *bugonia* in 4, Palinurus in *Aen*. 5, Marcellus in 6, Camilla in 11); integration of episodes both into individual books (the loss of Eurydice contrasts with the regeneration of bees in the *bugonia* as Aristaeus realizes that Orpheus' tragedy sprang from his failure to observe divine commands like those Proserpina will give him; Aeneas finally realizes, in the Creusa interview, that it is the divine command that he leave Troy) and into their poems as a whole (Eurydice shares features of Proserpina in *Geo*. 1, the idea of resurrection occurs in the first line of *Geo*. 3, Johnston (Ch. II, n. 112), 161-172); the loss of Creusa makes Aeneas all the more vulnerable, if not available, to Dido who is likewise recently widowed; Eurydice must die so that the new hive of bees can be begun in a foreign land; Creusa must die so that a new Troy can be begun in a foreign land. Within these correspondences Virgil has adapted the earlier episode with changes occasioned by the development

It is thus clear that Virgil had taken the received versions of the Orpheus-myth, added to them the vain grasping at a phantom, perhaps from the interview of Achilles and the ghost of Patroclus in *Il.* 23.62-107 (esp. 99-101) and that of Odysseus and the ghost of his mother in *Od.* 11.152-224 (esp. 204-209) and created an epic episode with which to conclude the *Georgics*. He then re-used the general structure and much of the language, stressing rather the Odyssean than Iliadic counterpart, in his treatment of the loss of Creusa. But he uses the same narrative structure once again in Book 2, without significant verbal repetition.

After Aeneas witnesses from the roof of the palace the death of Priam and his sons, he is seized by a *horror*. His own family appear to him in a vision and he starts back to find them. He is interrupted when he catches sight of Helen crouching in a recess of the shrine of Vesta. Whether or not the Helen Episode (567-587) is Virgilian is a problematical question. Most scholars agree that the ensuing interview with Venus is authentic.[5] She appears to him, reproaches then comforts him, and finally vanishes, having informed her son that there is no salvation for the present situation at Troy. The events leading up to the meeting with Venus (terror at the fall of Troy, concern for family) are similar to those preceding the interview with Creusa and seem to be further evidence against the authenticity of the meeting with Helen.[6]

---

of his style (e.g. *integrat* in *Geo.* 4.515 is altered to *ingeminans*, a more correct word, in *Aen.* 2.771) and the requirements of the narrative (e.g. Orpheus loses Eurydice by looking back too soon, Aeneas loses Creusa by not looking back soon enough; Orpheus dies as a (delayed) result of his loss, while Aeneas goes on to greater glory. Eurydice's tone of bitter rebuke and eternal woe is short (494-498) and is the catalyst for Orpheus' wild emotional response; Creusa's initial remonstrance is followed by a comforting reassurance that the gods have ordained this seeming tragedy and that a happy and glorious life will eventually be his (776-789). Aeneas' response to this rather cold comfort is briefly emotional, but he quickly gathers his men and sets out for Troy).

[5] Authentic, if unfinished. Henry felt that it was added by Virgil to smooth the transition from 567-624. For an historical account of opinions on this passage and a considered judgement of its validity, see G. P. Goold, "Servius and the Helen Episode", *HSCP* 74 (1970), 155-160.

[6] vv. 752-770 show Aeneas searching for Creusa, his panic growing as he sees the Greeks despoiling Troy and leading off captives. His encounter with Creusa's shade is thus well prepared-for. The entire passage from the witnessing of Priam's death to the departure of Venus represents the gradual realization that the gods are aligned against Troy. It rises "to a loud cre-

In the following chart, the first episode (the events following Priam's death and the subsequent confrontation with Venus) are outlined on the left side of the page, the events in the "loss of Creusa" episode are on the right. The parallels between these two series of events and the Eurydice tale have already been made clear. I did not include the interview with Venus in my earlier discussion because of a lack of verbal parallels.

| *Aen.* 2.559-633 | *Aen.* 2.732-804 |
|---|---|
| *horror* seizes Aeneas (559) | *male numen amicum* |
| Anchises appears (560) | Anchises appears (732-733) |
| Creusa appears (562) | Creusa disappears (738-739) |
| Aeneas looks back (564) | Aeneas does not look back (740) |
| | Aeneas turns back (749-751) |

| HELEN EPISODE | |
|---|---|
| Venus appears (589) | Creusa appears (773) |
| Venus reproaches (594-595) | Creusa reproaches (776-777) |
| Venus prophesies (596-619) | Creusa prophesies (777-784) |
| Venus comforts (620) | Creusa comforts (783-788) |
| Venus vanishes (621) | Creusa vanishes (791) |
| Aeneas returns to gather family (624ff.) | Aeneas returns to gather companions (796ff.) |

We can see that Virgil has taken the structure of the "loss of Eurydice" episode from the fourth *Georgic* and used it not once but twice in two parallel incidents in *Aeneid* 2. These incidents serve both the empathetic feeling-tone of the book, in that they elaborate the sense of irretrievable loss in Troy's destruction, and they serve the needs of the narrative in that both motivate Aeneas to leave Troy.

The Homeric paradigm for the scene with Venus is Achilles' meeting with his divine mother in *Il.* 1.413-427, in which she prophesies the outcome of the Trojan War and her son's death. To this we may also add Odysseus' interview with his mother in the Underworld, *Od.* 11.152-156, in which Anticleia tells him of the situation at Ithaca and of her own death (180-203). From this scene (204-209) Virgil may also have taken the vain grasping at the phantom that he uses in the Eurydice and Creusa episodes. He

---

scendo" which is pointlessly interrupted by the Helen Episode (Goold, ibid.). "To Aeneas, as he appears in the Helen Episode, Venus' line of argument is irrelevant". (ibid., 157)

also adds the messages of comfort spoken by the apparitions and extends and specifies the prophecy. To the basic structure of the Eurydice tale he adds several verbal parallels: Creusa fills the house with crying (*implere*).[7] Aeneas vainly cries for Creusa (768-770), the young boys and old women in Troy observe (765-766), as opposed to the boys and unwed maidens in Hades (476). In addition, Virgil includes the fire imagery so prominent in the book (and perhaps recalled by the smoke-simile at Creusa's evaporation).

Each of these three episodes climax in the confrontation of a valiant and loving hero with a woman who cannot save the situation his temporary madness has caused. Both poems go on, at greatly different lengths and by very different means, to show the resolution of such kinds of madness.

As I have mentioned, there are, despite the structural similarities, few verbal parallels between Aeneas' interviews with his mother and his wife, or even between the meeting with Venus and the Eurydice tale, although in each case the relationship and influence are clear. This kind of deliberate variation of obvious repetition is, as we have seen, characteristic of Virgil.

A concise general statement of the nature of Virgil's poetic innovation might be that he transformed every genre he worked in. He added to the timeless pastorals of Theocritus, the dour didactics of Hesiod, and the majestic, archaic epics of Homer the stamp of an Augustanism, at first hopeful, later serenely confident. With a conservative modernity he was able to wed the poetic taste of his time to the greatest models of ancient Greece and thus to bring forth unique works which evoke out of time a special era. The means at his genius' disposal were manifold and not the least of them was the continuation of certain themes throughout his poems. One, as I have said, is his Augustanism. Another is his personal conception of nature as a vivid, sentient universe, the daily workings of whose elements display and reflect a broad range of human experience. If this conception of nature is expressed with a greater strength and sympathy in the *Aeneid* than in the *Georgics*, it is due as much to a refined skill in using his similes and descriptions as to a deeper, more mature sensibility.

If, as I have tried to show, Virgil had no models for many of

---

[7] Compare the Dryads filling the mountains with weeping in *Geo.* 4.460-461, an echo of Orpheus' lamentation.

the specific themes common to both poems, he had no imitators. We have no works from antiquity that are at once so different and so similar as Virgil's, partly because of the sheer power of his influence which, like the wave in *Georgics* 3, overcame everything it encountered.

So; Virgil used his own works, borrowed from them, adapted from them, altered them, sometimes obviously, sometimes imperceptibly, in a manner and to an extent unique in ancient literature. In addressing the questions of source and technique, this study may provide a point from which the greater question, that of the development of Virgil's poetic style through all his works, may begin.

# BIBLIOGRAPHY

Following is a list of works cited in the text.

## I. TEXTS AND COMMENTARIES

*Fragmenta Comicorum Graecorum*, ed. A. Meineke, I, Berlin, 1970.
*Rhetores Graeci*, ed. L. von Spengel, II, Leipzig, 1854.
Virgil, *P. Vergili Maronis Aeneidos Liber Primus*, ed. R. G. Austin, Oxford, 1971.
——. *P. Vergili Maronis Aeneidos Liber Quartus*, ed. R. G. Austin, Oxford, 1955.
——. *P. Vergili Maronis Aeneidos Liber Quartus*, ed. A. S. Pease, Cambridge, Mass., 1935.
——. *P. Vergili Maronis Aeneidos Liber Secundus*, ed. R. G. Austin, Oxford, 1964.
——. *P. Vergili Maronis Aeneidos Liber Sextus*, ed. R. G. Austin, Oxford, 1977.
——. *P. Vergili Maronis Bucolica et Georgica*, ed. T. E. Page, London, 1898.
——. *P. Vergili Maronis Opera*, ed. R. A. B. Mynors, Oxford, 1969.
——. *P. Vergili Maronis Opera*, ed. M. Geymonat, Turin, 1973.
——. *P. Vergili Maronis Opera: The Works of Virgil*, ed. J. Conington; vol. iii, 3rd ed., rev. by H. Nettleship, London, 1883.
——. *The Aeneid of Virgil*, ed. J. Mackail, Oxford, 1930.
——. *The Aeneid of Virgil Books 1-6*, ed. R. D. Williams, London, 1972.
——. *Vergil Georgica*, ed. W. Richter, Munich, 1957.
——. *Virgil: Georgics I and IV*, ed. H. H. Huxley, London, 1963.

## II. BOOKS

Axelson, B., *Unpoetische Wörter*, Lund, 1945.
Böckh, A., *Graecae Tragoediae Principium*, Heidelburg, 1808.
Bowra, C. M., *Tradition and Design in the Iliad*, Oxford, 1930.
Büchner, K., *P. Vergilius Maro, Der Dichter der Römer*, Stuttgart, 1966. (= *RE* VIIIA, cols. 1021ff.).
Cruttwell, R., *Virgil's Mind at Work*, New York, 1969.
Fowler, W. W., *The Death of Turnus*, Oxford, 1919.
Fraenkel, E., *Horace*, Oxford, 1957.
George, E. V., *Aeneid VIII and the Aitia of Callimachus*, Leiden, 1974.
Gladow, F., *De Vergilio ipsius imitatore*, Dissertation Greifswald, 1921.
Glass, M., *The Fusion of Stylistic Elements in Vergil's Georgics*, Dissertation, Columbia, New York, 1913.
Guillemin, A. M., *L'Originalité de Virgile: étude sur la méthode littéraire antique*, Paris, 1931.
Heinze, R., *Virgils epische Technik*, 3rd ed., Berlin, 1915.
Henselmann, V., *Die Widerspruche in Vergils Aeneis*, Würzburg, 1914.
Hornsby, R. A., *Patterns of Action in the Aeneid*, Iowa City, 1970.
Johnson, W. R., *Darkness Visible: A Study of Vergil's Aeneid*, Berkeley, 1976.
Kann, S., *De iteratis apud poetas antiquae et mediae comoediae Atticae*, Gissen, 1909.

Klingner, F., *Virgil: Bucolica, Georgica, Aeneis*, Zurich & Stuttgart, 1967.
Knight, W. F. J., *Roman Vergil*, London, 1966.
Lee, D. J. N., *The Similes of the Iliad and Odyssey Compared*, Melbourne, 1964.
Matsen, P. P., *Hesiod's Works and Days and Homeric Oral Poetry*, Dissertation, Bryn Mawr, 1969.
Moskalew, W., *Verbal Repetition in Vergil's Aeneid*, Dissertation Yale, New Haven, 1975.
Mylius, K., *Die wiederholten Verse bei Vergil*, Dissertation Freiburg, 1946.
Newton, F. L., *Studies in Verbal Repetition in Virgil*, Dissertation, North Carolina, Chapel Hill, 1953.
Otis, B., *Virgil: A Study in Civilized Poetry*, Oxford, 1963.
Page, D., *Actors Interpolations in Greek Tragedy*, Oxford, 1934.
Perret, J., *Virgile: l'homme et l'oeuvre*, Paris, 1967.
Pöschl, V., *The Art of Virgil: Image and Symbol in the Aeneid*, tr. G. Seligson, Ann Arbor, 1962.
Putnam, M. C. J., *The Poetry of the Aeneid*, Cambridge, Mass., 1965.
Quinn, K., *Vergil's Aeneid: A Critical Description*, Ann Arbor, 1968.
Reiff, A., *Interpretatio, imitatio, aemulatio: Begriff und Vorstellung literarischer Abhängigkeit bei den Römern*, Dissertation Cologne, Würzburg, 1959.
Roiron, F. X.-J., *Étude sur l'imagination auditive de Virgile*, Paris, 1909.
Schadewaldt, W., *Iliasstudien*, ASAW 43, 6, Leipzig, 1938.
Sellar, W. Y., *The Roman Poets of the Augustan Age: Virgil*, Oxford, 1877.
Sparrow, J., *Half-Lines and Repetitions in Virgil*, Oxford, 1931.
Strassburger, G., *Die kleinen Kämpfer der Ilias*, Dissertation Frankfurt, 1954.
Walbank, F. W., *Speeches in the Greek Historians*, Oxford, 1966.
Wigodsky, M., *Vergil and Early Latin Poetry*, Wiesbaden, 1972.
Wilkinson, L. P., *The Georgics of Virgil*, Cambridge, 1969.
Williams, G., *Tradition and Originality in Roman Poetry*, Oxford, 1968.

## III. ARTICLES

Albrecht, E., "Wiederholte Verse und Versteile bei Vergil", *Hermes* 16 (1881), 393-444.
Anderson, W. S., "Vergil's Second *Iliad*", *TAPA* 88 (1957), 17-30.
Arend, W., "Die typischen Szenen bei Homer", *Problemata* 7 (1933).
Bayet, J., "Les Premiers 'Géorgiques' de Virgile", *RPh* 56 (1930), 128-150, 227-247.
Cahen, R., "Pour Virgile", *REG* 45 (1932), 1-6.
Clarke, R. J., "Two Virgilian Similes and the *Herakleos Katabasis*", *Phoenix* 24 (1970), 244-255.
Coleiro, E., "Allegory in the IVth Georgic", *Vergiliana: Recherches sur Virgile*, ed. H. Bardon & R. Verdière, Leiden, 1971, 113-123.
Cook, A. B., "Unconscious Iterations", *CR* 16 (1902), 146-158, 256-267.
Dahlmann, H., "Der Bienenstaat in Vergils *Georgica*", *Abh. Akad. Mainz, Geistesw. Kl.* 1954, 547-562.
Drew, D. L., "The Structure of Vergil's *Georgics*", *AJP* 50 (1929), 242-254.
Fenik, B., "Parallelism of Theme and Imagery in *Aeneid* II and IV", *AJP* 80 (1959), 1-24.
Ferguson, J., "Fire and Wound: the Imagery of *Aeneid* iv.1ff.", *PVS* 10 (1970-1971), 57-63.
Friederich, W. H., *Verwundung und Tod in der Ilias*, *Abh. Akad. Gött. Phil.-Hist.*, 3 (1956).

Friedländer, P., Δὶς καὶ τρὶς τὸ καλόν'', TAPA 69 (1938), 375-380.

Getty, R., "Some Astronomical Cruces in the Georgics", TAPA 79 (1948), 24-45.

Goold, G. P., "Servius and the Helen Episode", HSCP 74 (1970), 101-168.

Grant, J., "Dido Melissa", Phoenix 23 (1969), 380-391.

Hardie, C., "The Georgics: A Transitional Poem", Third Jackson Knight Memorial Lecture, Berkshire, 1971.

Hartigan, K. V., " 'He Rose Like a Lion...': Animal Similes in Homer and Virgil", AAntHung 21 (1973), 223-244.

Herrmann, L., "Le quatrième livre des Géorgiques et les abeilles d'Actium", REA 33 (1931), 219-224.

Heurgon, J., "Un exemple peu connu de la retractatio virgilienne", REL 9 (1931), 258-268.

Hough, J. N., "Bird Imagery in Roman Poetry", CJ 79 (1974), 1-13.

Jahn, P., "Aus Vergils Dichterwerkstätte (Georgica III.49-470)" RhM 60 (1905), 361-387.

Johnston, P. A., "Eurydice and Proserpina in the Georgics", TAPA 107 (1977), 161-172.

Knox, B. M. W., "The Serpent and the Flame: The Imagery of the Second Book of the Aeneid", AJP 71 (1950), 379-400.

Kraggerud, E., "Vergil über die Gründung Kartagos", SO 38 (1963), 32-37.

Leach, E. W., "Sedes Apibus from the Georgics to the Aeneid", Vergilius 23 (1977), 2-20.

Liebeschuetz, W., "Beast and Man in the Third Book of Virgil's Georgics", G & R 12 (1965), 64-77.

Lloyd-Jones, H., "Heracles at Eleusis P. Oxy. 2622 and P.S.I. 1391", Maia 19 (1967), 206-229.

Lyne, R. O. A. M., " 'Scilicet et tempus veniet...' Virgil, Geo. 1.463-514", Quality and Pleasure in Latin Poetry, ed. T. Woodman and D. West, Cambridge, 1974, 47-66.

McKay, A. J., review of Hornsby, AJP 94 (1973), 317.

Miller, W., "Repetition of Lines in Aristophanes", AJP 65 (1944), 26-36.

Moseley, N., "The Repeated Lines of Virgil", TAPA 52 (1922), xx.

Newton, F. L., "Recurrent Imagery in Aeneid 4", TAPA 88 (1957), 31-43.

Otis, B., "Virgilian Narrative in the Light of Its Precursors and Successors", SPh 73 (1976), 1-28.

Perkins, J., "An Aspect of Latin Comparison Construction", TAPA 104 (1974), 261-277.

Reckford, K. J., "Some Trees in Virgil and Tolkien", Perspectives of Roman Poetry: A Classics Symposium, ed. G. K. Galinsky, Austin, Texas, 1974, 57-91.

Reinhardt, K., "Der Schild der Achilles", Freundesgabe für E. R. Curtius, Berne, 1956.

Richards, G. C., "Cicero", Oxford Classical Dictionary, Oxford, 1968, 190.

Segal, C. P., " 'Like Winds and Winged Dream': A Note on Virgil's Development", CJ 69 (1973-1974), 97-101.

Thaniel, G., "Vergil's Leaf-and-Bird Similes of Ghosts", Phoenix 25 (1971), 237-245.

Verral, M. deG., "Two Instances of Symbolism in the Sixth Aeneid", CR 24 (1910), 43-46.

Vischi, L., "Similitudini virgiliane", C & N 5 (1909), 235-246.

Wilkins, E. G., "A Classification of the Similes in the Argonautica of Apollonius Rhodius", CW 14 (1921), 162-166.

# INDEX LOCORUM

Printed in the United States
By Bookmasters